Curriculum Studies in the United States

DOI: 10.1057/9781137303424

Other Palgrave Pivot titles

palgrave▸pivot

Curriculum Studies in the United States: Present Circumstances, Intellectual Histories

William F. Pinar

palgrave
macmillan

DOI: 10.1057/9781137303424

CURRICULUM STUDIES IN THE UNITED STATES
Copyright © William F. Pinar, 2013.

First published in 2013 by
PALGRAVE MACMILLAN®
in the United States—a division of St. Martin's Press LLC,
175 Fifth Avenue, New York, NY 10010.

Where this book is distributed in the UK, Europe and the rest of the world,
this is by Palgrave Macmillan, a division of Macmillan Publishers Limited,
registered in England, company number 785998, of Houndmills,
Basingstoke, Hampshire RG21 6XS.

Palgrave Macmillan is the global academic imprint of the above companies
and has companies and representatives throughout the world.

Palgrave® and Macmillan® are registered trademarks in the United States,
the United Kingdom, Europe and other countries.

ISBN: 978-1-137-30343-1 EPUB
ISBN: 978-1-137-30342-4 PDF
ISBN: 978-1-137-30341-7 Hardback

Library of Congress Cataloging-in-Publication Data is available from the
Library of Congress.

A catalogue record of the book is available from the British Library.

First edition: 2013

www.palgrave.com/pivot

DOI: 10.1057/9781137303424

Contents

DOI: 10.1057/9781137303424

palgrave▶pivot

www.palgrave.com/pivot

DOI: 10.1057/9781137303424

Introduction

Abstract: *I define the key concepts—present circumstances, intellectual history—and explain the significance of their juxtaposition. After reminding readers of my qualifications that make me eligible to undertake the study, I conclude with a summary of what is to follow in chapters 1–3 and the Epilogue.*

Pinar, F. William. *Curriculum Studies in the United States: Present Circumstances, Intellectual Histories.* New York: Palgrave Macmillan, 2013. DOI: 10.1057/9781137303424.

▶

> [W]e all speak and write within heritages which produce us as much as we produce them.
>
> Dennis Carlson (2010, 204)

The deliberate destruction of public education summarizes the immediate and local external circumstances in which Americans work.[1] For a field that once had professional jurisdiction over public-school curriculum development, this is a catastrophe and on several fronts. Witnessing the destruction of the public school is horrific enough. At some subliminal level there must be profound frustration, and if not self-blame, then at least some degree of self-dissociation. The inability of the field to intervene in so-called school reform[2] undermines any sense of professional or individual agency[3]. Add to these present conditions an open skepticism toward curriculum studies—which, as Tom Barone (2010, 477) knows, "rightfully lies at the heart of education"—by some in other specializations of the academic field of education. Always confident that education is a quantifiable problem, these "colleagues"—with their uninformed fantasies of "evidence-based" research[4]—capitalize on the federal government's demands that educational research answer the (inadequate[5]) classroom question "what works?" Those who claim to know "what works" demand control of teacher education, just as it threatens to be dissolved by politicians determined to privatize the preparation of teachers (see Ravitch 2012).

Many curriculum-studies scholars work in teacher education programs. That was my experience.[6] In many states, teacher education has already been undermined, with reduced coursework required for certification. Faced with skepticism if not outright hostility as they watch the destruction of the institution to which most hold profound conceptual allegiance—the constructs of the "public school" and of "childhood-as-rescue" (Baker (2010, 345)—curriculum-studies scholars working in the United States face a nightmarish present and an uncertain future.[7]

A decade ago I began a sequel[8] to *Understanding Curriculum* (Pinar et al. 1995)—a mapping of the US field after its 1970s Reconceptualization[9]—but abandoned the project due to the demands of the new position. Moving meant not only institutional demands but numerous opportunities afforded by working in Canada,[10] opportunities simultaneously intellectual (Pinar 2011c) and financial (e.g. research funding provided by Ottawa). I had ended my sojourn in the United States focused on race (2006b)– as perhaps the central subject in American public life and a

DOI: 10.1057/9781137303424

provocation to reconceptualize curriculum development.[11] That theoretical and practical labor compelled considerations of the discipline.[12] I proposed two structures of disciplinarity that could support intellectual advancement: *verticality* and *horizontality*, e.g. studies in the intellectual history of the field and analyses of its present circumstances (Pinar 2007).

Like the discipline of intellectual history (see Pinar 2006a, 1–14), *verticality* documents the ideas that constitute the complicated conversation[13] that is an academic discipline. "[I]f the tendency is now to associate interdisciplinarity with freedom, and disciplinarity with constraint," Amanda Anderson and Joseph Valente (2002, 2) point out, a "closer look at the history of these disciplines shows that the dialectic of agency and determinism, currently distributed across the disciplinary/interdisciplinary divide, was at the heart of disciplinary formation itself." That "dialectic of agency and determinism" is discernible in the *Handbook of Curriculum Studies: The Next Moment*, the sourcebook for my speculations here concerning the paradigmatic shift I suspect is now underway. That "dialectic" occurs within the intellectual history of the field and the press of its present circumstances. Studies in the intellectual history of the field must be supplemented by sustained attention to present circumstances. The second disciplinary structure the cultivation of which can contribute to the field's intellectual advancement is, then, *horizontality*.

Horizontality references the field's present set of intellectual circumstances—the concepts that structure disciplinary conversation now—but as well the political situation that influences and, all too often, structures these concepts. "This effort to name and construct and cohere the world that matters," Lyn Yates and Madeleine Grumet (2011, 239) explain, referencing the school curriculum, "does not take place on some idealized plane, but is constantly informed by and reacting to events. This world that emerges from curriculum is always in conversation with the world outside schooling." The same reciprocal relation obtains between the world and the academic field that studies the school curriculum.

To convey the political situation, I turn to newspaper reports from late 2011 and early 2012.[14] Whether or not they see *The New York Times* (my primary source), US teachers have heard the news. According to the annual MetLife Survey of the American Teacher, morale among the nation's teachers has now fallen to its lowest point in more than 20 years. More than half of teachers surveyed expressed at least some reservation about their jobs. One in three teachers admitted they were likely to leave

DOI: 10.1057/9781137303424

the profession in the next five years. Just three years ago, the rate had been one in four. In addition to decreased budgets[15] accompanying the Great Recession, there are other causes of teachers' demoralization, Santos (2012, March 8, A15) reports, chief among them demands for increased assessment as well as the devaluation of seniority. "Seniority" is a term politicians often associate with union contracts and not with the professional wisdom, erudition, and practical judgment that can come with professional experience (see Henderson and Kesson 2003).[16]

There are other insidious developments that undermine the profession of teaching in the United States. Teaching-to-the-test positions technology—not the student, not the professional educator—as central to educational experience. In research conducted by economists, the teacher's role is rendered important only insofar as it raises students' scores on standardized exams.[17] Not all teachers accept this nonsense. From Idaho we learn of one teacher's affirmation of the centrality of teachers' intellectual engagement with students—not technology—to teaching and learning. Other reports document the plundering of public budgets by private companies.[18] These developments, as I will suggest, underscore the inadequacy of the concept of "power"—both its "reproduction" and our "resistance" to it—in understanding curriculum today.

Next I will turn to a review of the key concepts of the reconceptualized field—power, discourse, identity—that have informed US efforts to understand curriculum. No longer specific interventions in a field first focused on procedure—the Tyler Rationale and its offspring—these concepts have faded into the background of what US-based scholars study today. Dereferentialized, they circulate as assumptions not arguments; without grounding they cannot articulate the specificity of the present moment. Like the proceduralism my generation challenged, the conceptual legacies of the reconceptualized field have now become the taken-for-granted assumptions that, for the field to advance intellectually, must be surpassed. These concepts once represented important advances in our efforts to understand curriculum. Now as background, as assumptions, their surpassing is now underway, and I rely on the 2010 *Handbook of Curriculum Studies* to reference how. The source is specific, I realize, and the hour is early; despite these limitations movement is discernible. This "next moment" of "post-reconceptualization" that the *Handbook* documents signals is a second paradigm shift in the US field. How this reconceptualization might proceed—in particular its relation

DOI: 10.1057/9781137303424

to internationalization—concludes this exercise in retrospection and speculation.

Internationalization

In the coming paradigm shift, internationalization can play an enabling role, providing both conceptual distance from the US field's present circumstances and intellectual histories, as well as provocations for reconstructing the canon and formulating new concepts. Indeed, it is through the internationalization of the field—accenting its cosmopolitan character—that Americans can accomplish the reconceptualization. Internationalization affords a cosmopolitan education ending the disabling provincialism accompanying American conceptions of their exceptionality. Study is key, and that concept signals the significance of specific traditions of those who were first identified—if negatively, as "rootless" (quoted in Pinar 2012, 96)—with cosmopolitanism, e.g. the Jews. From a model of Torah-study associated with this simultaneously national and international people—it is a model that affirms the intersection of intellectual histories with present circumstances—US scholars can undertake the reconceptualization of curriculum studies.

It is a version of that model I employ in ongoing secular international studies. Laboring to understand our colleagues, work worldwide is intrinsically important, but, I argue, these studies also demonstrate the paradigmatic possibility of a more cosmopolitan conception of curriculum studies in the United States. During 2006–2010 I completed studies of the intellectual histories and present circumstances of three nationally distinctive fields: Brazil, Mexico, and South Africa (Pinar 2010, 2011b, 2011d). Why those three nations? While in the general terms each of these nations is significant in the North American imaginary, in specific terms the concepts these fields have formulated provide important contrasts to those concepts now fading into the background in the US. While these cannot be imported like "raw materials" for conceptual "distribution" in the US, they can be recontextualized, enabling US scholars to rethink their assumptions. As an example, I will reference Elizabeth Macedo's conception of "enunciation," both to contrast the situation in Brazil and the United States, and recontextualize it in my assertion of agency over reproduction.

DOI: 10.1057/9781137303424

Globalization was well underway when William Reynolds, Patrick Slattery, Peter Taubman and I were depicting that last paradigm shift, and one chapter in it is devoted to understanding curriculum as international text (Pinar et al. 1995, 792–843). Twenty years ago international studies seemed supplemental, not integral, to the reconceptualization of curriculum studies in the United States, even though its key concepts had been imported from Great Britain (Pinar 2011a, 27).[19] While for many Americans September 11, 2001 remains the moment of demarcation, scholars almost everywhere else have been clear that the concept of the global village—the creation of Marshall McLuhan, that great Canadian theorist of the electronic era—has indeed materialized. The present circumstances of almost every academic field is simultaneously national, regional, and global.

The world at risk (to invoke Ulrich Beck's phrasing) demands our sustained attention, but necessity is not the only mother of invention. The cosmopolitan[20] cause of curriculum studies calls upon us to contradict the inevitable provincialism of knowing only one's own field. Because history renders present circumstances intelligible, internationalization affirms not only horizontality—ongoing analyses of present circumstances—but verticality (e.g. historicality) as well. Conceptualization requires referentialization, e.g. linking concepts to the extra-discursive circumstances of their formulation, contextualizing them in various histories, specifying their meanings, considering their consequences. While one needs no justification to study curriculum studies in Brazil, Mexico, and South Africa—these are fascinating fields, important on their own terms—I reference them here as their intellectual histories and present circumstances also function to recontextualize the concepts that US curricularists invoke to face the challenges of the present moment.

Then and now

The US field's external circumstances today are not entirely different from those in 1970 when Joseph Schwab asserted that the field was moribund. The internal circumstances of the field are quite different today. Then Schwab was postulating his structures-of-the-disciplines theory—in alignment with the Kennedy Administration's national curriculum reform—while Dwayne Huebner (1999) and James B. Macdonald (1995) were undertaking an analysis of the very language of the curriculum field. Daniel and Laurel Tanner were criticizing the militarization of

DOI: 10.1057/9781137303424

curriculum reform that the Sputnik incident had triggered (see Pinar et al. 1995, 161). Herbert Kliebard (2000 [1970]a) was underscoring the ameliorative and ahistorical orientation of the field and preparing his definitive critique of Tyler's four questions (Kliebard 2000 [1970]b). Where the field would go—if anywhere, warned Schwab in 1970—was not obvious.

Four decades later US scholars face not "reform" but the actual hijacking of the US public-school curriculum, this time by computer-company profiteers. This time the US field faces the intellectual exhaustion of its key concepts, most conspicuously "reproduction" and "resistance." New concepts are required for the reconstruction of curriculum studies in the United States, but these be found not in the present, but in the field's past, and not only there. This time the future of the US field may not be found in the US at all, but elsewhere, both geographically and culturally. Before I turn to the hijacking of the US public-school curriculum, I will focus on the conceptual depletion[21] within the field itself. Both sets of present circumstances support a second paradigmatic shift in the field.

To point out that the primary sectors of scholarship in the US field— efforts focused on power, identity, and discourse—are exhausted is not criticism but, rather, acknowledgment of their success. Their basic assumptions—that power predominates, that identity is central, and that discourse is determinative (e.g. our research provides only narratives, never truth)—are widely shared. While each conception of curriculum is in tension with the other, the three share the same tendency toward totalization. Power, identity, and discourse are no longer conceptual innovations or provocations precisely due to their taken-for-grantedness. As assumptions, these concepts circulate as accepted truth—even the poststructuralist truth that there is no truth!—and have thus become abstractions split-off from the concrete complexity of the historical moment. Split-off, they do not link us to the present and can no longer provide passages to the future. In their triumph they become markers of our defeat: our expulsion from the public sphere.

That sequence specifies the process of conceptual exhaustion. While always situated within and derived from ongoing conversation, new concepts[22] arise in response to immediate sometimes novel but often recurring problems, enduring but perhaps now mesmerizing mysteries, and unexpected possibly counter-intuitive facts. (I acknowledge the blurred boundaries among these three as well as other sources and provocations of concepts.) New concepts can be extensions of extant concepts but not

DOI: 10.1057/9781137303424

mere imitations. When extensions they are not exactly new concepts, but subspecies of extant concepts that pinpoint something previously overlooked. In Kuhn's (1962) terms, the former lies in the realm of so-called normal science, and the latter could signal a shift in paradigms. Counter-paradigmatic evidence, facts that fail to fit extant theories, and/or new theories that open for study new phenomena or recast old ones, create the conditions for reconceptualization.

In general terms this describes the situation in US curriculum studies after the national school reform of the 1960s. No longer were there conditions in place to support the institutional curriculum development Tyler's principles had organized. It was not only this scheme—which links outcomes to objectives, recasting teaching as implementation—that was to blame for the loss of professional agency, setting the stage for four decades of "school reform." It was this cataclysmic shift in the once close relationship between university-based professors and the public schools that forced the 1970s Reconceptualization of curriculum studies in the United States. Because institutional curriculum development was no longer the province of education professors, I proposed that the field focus on understanding curriculum. While many refused to face the new reality or align themselves with the concept, within a decade the US field had been reconceptualized from school-based curriculum development to theoretically-informed efforts to make sense of what had happened and is happening now in schools (see Pinar et al. 1995).

Probably due to this startling exercise of power in separating schools from education professors, one of the first efforts to understand curriculum was focused on the political. The key concept that informed this theory-based research was reproduction, to be followed not ten years later by resistance (Pinar et al. 1995, 253). *Contra* to the common sense of the time, reproduction theorists argued that schools do not provide opportunities for upward social and economic mobility. On the contrary, they argued that schools reproduced power through ideological control of the curriculum. By the end of the 1970s it was dawning on these theorists that such a totalizing conception left little room for change, and so the concept of "resistance" was embraced. In the 1970s and early 1980s there was excitement associated with these ideas: they had overturned a previously held assumption about schools (that they were avenues of upward social and economic mobility), communicated the calamity that had befallen the field (that university-based professors no longer enjoyed

DOI: 10.1057/9781137303424

professional jurisdiction over the school curriculum), and affirmed their determination to oppose it. But the two concepts—reproduction and resistance—positioned theorists outside the world they claimed to see so clearly. It was a world they were, as spectators, helpless to change. The very scale of their analysis ensured that incremental change was discredited as tinkering. Nothing less than "radical" and systemic change would suffice. Even if curriculum-studies professors had been able to encourage incremental change, it is unclear if they could not have altered the course of US school reform during the final decades of the twentieth century. But such engagement with the everyday life of school—what in Brazil is research on the quotidian (see Pinar 2011b, 43–54, 93–114, 155–170)— would have linked abstractions to concrete circumstances and situations. Ethnography[23] became the accepted means to achieve that link, but ethnography often failed to improve either the situation researchers studied or contributed to any conceptual innovations.[24]

Once controversial and innovative interventions, "reproduction" and "resistance" are no longer controversial concepts. Indeed, they have faded—through their acceptance—into the background of what we think. That power predominates is a maxim now fused with our everyday assumptions, or "tacit ground" in Bohm's (1996, ix) terms. As background, they have become detached from the circumstances that once accorded them immediacy, that four decades ago enabled them to "ring true." Dereferentialized, they communicate nothing concrete. Because they are totalizing, everything we see and experience seems absorbed by them. If power predominates, passivity follows, as resistance becomes quixotic. The sequence becomes a self-absorbing obsession with what cannot, in its present conceptual form, be overcome. What is needed are concepts that convey what we experience now. These new concepts will come from studying the intellectual history of the field worldwide while attuned to present circumstances.

Notes

1   Such a claim can seem hyperbolic, but even former school reformer Diane Ravitch (see 2012, 40, emphasis added), discussing Mitt Romney's and Barack Obama's education policies, notes that "Restoring the promise of American education should mean rejuvenating public schools, not *destroying* them." One part of the platform to destroy public education

in America—destroy it, as we will see, by "privatizing" it, e.g. relocating curriculum and teaching to the province of profit-driven corporations—is by destroying the profession of teaching. While the Romney campaign proposes to end teacher certification (see Ravitch 2012), the Obama Administration has proposed a $5 billion competition aimed at destroying how America's teachers are prepared, paid and granted tenure. Ignorant of long-standing efforts to improve the intellectual quality of teacher education, critics allege that "colleges of education... [are guilty of] unfocused curriculum and weak entrance and graduation requirements" (Banchero 2012, February 15, A3). How colleges of education could have achieved either after decades of sustained political assault from politicians and on occasion from within universities themselves (from arts and sciences colleagues and administrators) is not obvious. Never mind the facts, approximately 25 US states are legislating that teacher education de-emphasize tests—somehow they remain appropriate for students but not their teachers—and written essays in favor of a less intellectually demanding, indeed bureaucratic (one might say "busywork) requirements. Rather than indications of their intellectual, e.g. professional, stature, aspiring teachers must submit lesson plans, homework assignments and videotaped versions of their teaching (Baker 2012, July 30, A1). Substituting bureaucratic for intellectual standards installs bureaucrats not teachers, and the prejudice toward "good looks" and assertive personalities will trump a teacher candidate's thoughtfulness, sensitivity, and erudition, none of which is necessarily visible on brief videotape. Critics have already pointed out the obvious, e.g. that this new assessment system cannot produce "better" teachers but only imposes a "standardized program" that undermines the academic freedom—the intellectual independence—of university faculty (Baker 2012, July 30, A3). Maria Neira, a vice president at New York State United Teachers, noted that this so-called reform was "driven by" politics and had excluded university faculty from even consultation: "It erodes the role of what professors do, which is create curriculum, create that coaching model," Neira reminded. "Who is going to grade the process? How will you ensure it will be done in a way that is far and equitable for all candidates?" One faculty member at a state university in New York quipped: "Our decisions are being outsourced" (quoted passages in Baker 2012, July 30, A3), referencing that videotapes, lessons plans and other documents will be examined by evaluators recruited by the education company Pearson. As we will see soon, privatization is in the service of profits, not professionalism. And as we will also see later in this essay, professionalism prompts protests. At the University of Massachusetts, Baker (2012, July 30, A3) reports, 67 of the 68 students preparing to become middle- and high-school teachers refused to submit two ten-minute videos of themselves teaching because, students complained, the evaluators chosen

DOI: 10.1057/9781137303424

by Pearson were "not qualified to judge their abilities, and should not be allowed to do so over their own professors." From the preparation of teachers to the classroom curriculum, school reform is school deform.

2　US school reform started as the displacement of blame for the 1957 Sputnik satellite launching (Pinar 2012, 104). Somehow the state of the schools was responsible for the failures of science, government, and the military-industrial complex. Curriculum reform also served to contain and redirect racialized and gendered resentments. By the 1980s political motives mixed with economic ones, and the "risk" (Beck 2009) at which schools were said to place the US was both political and economic (Pinar 2012, 200–202). Pointedly Peter Taubman (2009, 138) exposes the ruse: "When was the last time anyone blamed business schools for the failing economy or corporate scandals?" There have been many analyses of this deception, but none of them improves on Peter Taubman's (see 2009, 144). University faculty outside schools and colleges of education have tended to remain silent or join in the fun. But, as Taubman (2009, 48–49) points out, this game is now coming to their town too.

3　"Stripped of autonomy and intentionality, emptied of inner life, reduced to conglomeration of skills that are employed in environments in order to stimulate predetermined responses," Peter Taubman (2009, 194) points out, "teachers can easily be replaced by bureaucrats, mechanics, or machines. Reduced to information and metacognitive skills, the curriculum lends itself to teacher-proof scripts." This is well underway, as the reports summarized in chapter 1 make clear.

4　Because these terms—evidence-based research, data driven, etc—circulate within the world of business and the learning sciences, Peter Taubman (2009, 6) points out, "they tie the educational reforms to these two fields—science and business." Taubman's verb is perhaps inadvertently appropriate, as science and business confine education against its will, ending its intellectual freedom, ensuring its devolution into indoctrination.

5　"The unrelenting focus on 'what works,'" as John Willinsky (2006, 141) appreciates, "needs to be set within a larger and ongoing public dialogue over the nature of learning and the hopes of education." Central to "dialogue, learning and hope" is the canonical curriculum question: *what knowledge is of most worth*? The answer is rarely instrumental knowledge, but, especially in our time, that knowledge only the humanities and the arts can provide. "For all of the attention I have brought in this book to increasing access to the sciences and social sciences," Willinsky 2006, 147) writes, "the case for access to the humanities also needs to be acknowledged." Indeed.

6　That experience (Pinar 2009a) has been very much informed by the 40-year mentorship of Paul R. Klohr. As Nancy Brooks (2010, 185) appreciates, Klohr's work "is perhaps written more in the hearts and minds of his

DOI: 10.1057/9781137303424

students than in print, but who has been nevertheless as influential in the field."

7 "The deintellectualization and ahistorical nature of education, Petra Munro Hendry (2011, 209) points out, "make the future devoid of a past."

8 Marla Morris (2001, 2006, 2008, 2009) took up the project after I abandoned it and, I understand, that as of this writing (August 2012) her study nears completion. While her work is not represented in the *Handbook of Curriculum Studies*—my sourcebook here—she did participate in the 2006 Purdue Conference from which Erik Malewski worked (see Malewski 2010, 534).

9 Remarkably, there are those who continue to dispute the very concept of reconceptualization but, tellingly, they do so without argument or evidence. Calling it a "tidy conceptualization," Hendry (2010, 498), claims the concept "dehistoricizes the field and constructs a narrative of identity in which there is a natural progression of evolution in which our identity as curriculum theorists can be clearly defined." How the argument made in *Understanding Curriculum*—specified in extensive reference to historical events and linked to specific intellectual histories in the field—can be converted to a tale of "natural progression" seems itself entirely fictional. Given the range of and differences among the discourses discussed in *Understanding Curriculum*—including gendered and historical discourses to which her own work has contributed immeasurably (see Munro 1999, Hendry 2011)—the question of "identity" is hardly obvious, stable, or reductively defined. Paraskeva (2011, 137) devotes several pages serializing others' failure to grasp the concept; he quotes Apple's rejection of the concept—it is, revealingly, temper tantrum-like, entirely without argument or evidence—but Paraskeva proceeds, as if quoting others' complaints could add up to anything but intellectual petulance. We "learn" that the reconceptualization of the field was "counter-cultural" (how I had hoped!), guilty of "running away from the problems of practice" (2011, 138)—recall the field was expelled from the school during the Kennedy curriculum reform: "practice" had "run away" from us!—as ignoring schools' association with the economy, bureaucracy, behaviorism, racism and sexism, and yes as even ahistorical (2011, 139). Each of these informs much of the scholarship of the reconceptualized field, as *Understanding Curriculum* documents in detail. After this litany Paraskeva (2011, 140) is reduced to asking: "reconceptualize what"? Having forgetting the referent—the curriculum field in the US—he is of course compelled to dismiss any idea of "post-reconceptualization" (2011, 141).

10 It must be acknowledged that in Canada too the corporate sector has often controlled the curriculum. Interestingly, however, George Tomkins (1986, 139) reports that while "businesspeople...sought practical educational reform...[but] not all were as hostile to traditional learning....The self-made

DOI: 10.1057/9781137303424

man or woman could be transformed by liberal studies into a less bumptious and more humane person with a mental discipline that would also contribute to commercial success." In contrast, the great George Grant regarded "businessmen [as]...benign in their intensions towards the [educational] institutions they served, nevertheless [they] pushed and pulled, caressed and bullied, to transform the university into an appropriate instrument to serve the needs of the progressive capitalist societies of North America" (Christian 1996, 136).

11 The destruction of conditions supporting institutional curriculum development—rendered a procedure by Ralph W. Tyler (1949)—provoked the first paradigmatic shift in US curriculum studies. Replacing curriculum development were efforts to understand curriculum (see Pinar et al. 1995; Marshall, Sears, Allen, Roberts, Schubert 2006 (1999). While participation in the decades-long paradigm shift had at the time seemed consuming enough, by 2000 I had come to the same conclusion that Peter Grimmett and Mark Halvorson (2010, 241) also reached, that in the "process of correctly moving the field of curriculum away from technical rationality to reconceptualize it as historical and contemporary discourses, Pinar et al. omitted to reconceptualize the process by which curriculum is created." While they withhold judgment on the value and success of my efforts to rehabilitate curriculum development (see Pinar 2001, 2006a and 2006b), Grimmett and Halvorson (2010, 256 n. 2) do acknowledge that work, including the central role of "juxtaposition" in assembling synoptic texts today. Grimmett-Halvorson are now engaged in a promising effort to rehabilitate the concept of curriculum design, itself also a casualty of the 1970s Reconceptualization.

12 Disciplinarity acknowledges that academic disciplines are in flux and sometimes fragile, as Amariglio, Resnick and Wolff (1993, 151) emphasize: "disciplines can be seen as in the process of always becoming other, of multiplying, of undoing their own limits, of fracturing, and even of collapsing. See in this way, a discipline, whether robust or fragile, is indeed always a transitory thing." Like lived experience, then, participation in an academic discipline requires reconstruction of one's intellectual history in response to ever-shifting present circumstances, what Dennis Carlson (2010, 204) calls "our capacity to reassemble ourselves." Subjective reconstruction, Stuart Murray (2010, 243) suggests, is "the eternal enterprise of self-fashioning, learning and relearning who and what we are, and how we relate to the world and to others in it.... [W]e are those beings who stand *in* relation to ourselves questioningly." Subjective and social reconstruction are reciprocal and parallel the processes of disciplinary advancement.

13 See Pinar 2012, 188–198. Not only the university-based academic discipline but the school classroom can be the site of such conversation, as Susan Jean Mayer (2012) details. To take another important example, James Henderson

DOI: 10.1057/9781137303424

and Kathleen Kesson (see Henderson 2010, 261) link "curriculum dialogue" and "self-examination" with a conception of "democratic educational experience." There are many antecedents of these conceptions of curriculum, including, evidently, Schwab. "By deliberation," Block (2004, 129) argues, "Schwab meant the active participation in meaningful conversation." Block (2004, 6) underscores that "Schwab argued strongly for the institution of discussion *as* curriculum, what Schwab defined as an engagement in thought and communication." Key to Block's brilliant rereading of the canonical curriculum theorist is his insight that "Joseph Schwab spoke, too, from a silenced and invisible Jewish tradition" (Block 2004, 7). Indeed, Block (2004, 9) argues that "the Rabbis' methods that serves as a context for Schwab's prescriptions and that it is the Rabbis' methods that Schwab urges as the basis and methods of curriculum." Referencing both Block and John Willinsky, I suggest in the epilogue that Jewish conceptions of "study" might prove pivotal in the cultivation of disciplinarity in curriculum studies. Block (2004, 30) is even blunter: "[T]here might be a renascence of the field of curriculum, a renewed capacity to contribute to the quality of American education when curriculum energies are infused with the discourses of Talmudic study."

14 In recent years I have juxtaposed "current events" with theoretical formulations, not to reduce one to the other, but to install a creative tension between the two domains. While I do think theory should address—and be addressed by—the world, that world is not only "current events" but intellectual histories as well. This way of "dating" the material—historicizing the curriculum in theoretical terms—is hardly original. Foucault's lectures at the Collège de France, Paras (2006, 2) points out, were "filled with references to current world events, to books that have recently come into print, and even to headlines from the morning's newspaper." In my simple scheme to support the disciplinarity of curriculum studies, such referentialization underscores the present circumstances in which scholars work.

15 Enrollment in nearly half of the nation's largest school districts," Rich (2012, July 24, A1) reports, "has dropped steadily over the last five years, triggering school closures that have destabilized neighborhoods, caused layoffs of essential staff and concerns in many cities that the students who remain are some of the neediest and most difficult to educate." Charter schools are partly to blame (see 2012, A1, A3).

16 "We must not be fooled into thinking the word 'wisdom' is soft," Mary Aswell Doll (2011, 108) admonishes. It involves remaining "open to unknowing," Petra Munro Hendry (2011, 206) reminds. What is wisdom? "Wisdom is the joining of past and present," Alan Block (2009, 88) suggests. We don't want them fused of course, but juxtaposed, a "tension" Block (2010, 523) thinks of as "potentially generative."

DOI: 10.1057/9781137303424

17   Standardization, Peter Taubman (2009, 61) points out, "erases the specificity, heterogeneity, and idiosyncrasy of location and of individuals' experiences." The apparently innocuous concept of "standards" ensures standardization, Taubman (2009, 113) notes, "since the moment we introduce the word 'standard' we necessarily introduce standardization." Knowledge of standardization's deleterious educational effects is not new of course, even if the phenomenon seems more intense now than ever before. Alan Block (2004, 34) reminds that Joseph Schwab saw "standardized education as antithetical not only to education, but to democracy as well." Taubman (2009, 58) appreciates that "the ... real purpose of tests is not to measure but to coerce and punish," an authoritarian agenda disguised as educational (see Pinar 2012, 2–3).

18   Joel Spring (2012, 122, 154ff) has provided a detailed map of the interlocking networks of profiteers and politicians determined to privatize public education in the United States.

19   Not only the key concepts of efforts to understand curriculum as political came from the U.K.; the only precedent I could find for understanding curriculum as autobiographical was also British (see Abbs 1974). British conceptual imports have been less generative in teacher education, as Grimmett and Young (2012, 30) remind: "North American thinking about accountability has been roundly affected by events in the U.K. . . . . [the main effect of which] was to de-theorize, de-critique and de-intellectualize teacher education."

20   "Living in a world where difference and contingency are permanent conditions," Greg Dimitriadis 2010, 471) acknowledges, "demands a kind of cosmopolitan disposition." For a review of the concept, see Spector 2011; see also Jupp 2012, Harvey 2009.

21   I use "exhaustion" to suggest that the success of these efforts—their widespread acceptance, their conversion from intervention to assumption—results in dereferentialization. There is no need to argue on their behalf, to specify their concrete manifestations, precisely because they are now assumed.

22   On occasion deconstruction risks dissolving concepts altogether, although Bernadette Baker reminds that there is another option, e.g. "conserve old concepts—such as the world, subject, self, other, language, discourse—while here and there denouncing their limits" (2009, xxxi). The conservation of concepts, if through their reconstruction, is my commitment, but conservation does not appeal to Baker.

23   It had been a breakthrough concept in the United States at one time: see Jackson 1968. See also Jackson 2012.

24   See, for instance, Pinar 2011a, 147–148, n. 8; for exceptions see Jewett 2008; Burke 2011.

DOI: 10.1057/9781137303424

1

Present Circumstances

Abstract: *I start this chapter with acknowledgment that economists have replaced educationists as the key players in contemporary educational research, citing the research of Raj Chetty and John N. Friedman of Harvard University and Jonah E. Rockoff of Columbia University. Focusing on the flaws of the research, I accent its political complicity with the privatization of public education, in which "brick-and-mortar" schools are dismissed as antiquated "twentieth-century" institutions unable to cope with twenty-first century's realities. When curriculum is moved online, students can remain at home, and teachers, with whom students may have no direct contact, act as auditors, with commensurately reduced wages and intellectual influence. I focus on K12 Inc., a publicly traded company that manages several such "schools," as well as Apple Computers' presence in one North Carolina "model school." I conclude with commentary on the state-wide protests of teachers in Idaho against the forced incursion of technology into their classrooms.*

Pinar, F. William. *Curriculum Studies in the United States: Present Circumstances, Intellectual Histories.* New York: Palgrave Macmillan, 2013. DOI: 10.1057/9781137303424.

> [D]isciplines are political structures that mediate crucially between the political economy and the production of knowledge.
>
> Timothy Lenoir (1993, 72)

In early 2012, economists[1] Raj Chetty and John N. Friedman of Harvard University and Jonah E. Rockoff of Columbia University reported the results of research in which they tracked 2.5 million students over 20 years. In their findings, Chetty, Friedman, and Rockoff ascribed astonishing power to elementary- and middle-school teachers whose students' standardized test scores had increased. Those teachers, the economists concluded (in the reporter's words), "had wide-ranging, lasting positive effects on those students' lives beyond academics, including lower teenage pregnancy rates and greater college matriculation and adult earnings" (Lowrey 2011, January 6, A1). All else being equal, the economists explained, students with one "excellent" teacher (defined as a teacher whose students' standardized test scores rose) for one year between fourth and eight grades would gain $4,600 in lifetime income, compared to students with similar demographics whose scores did not increase (presumably because their teacher was "average"). Students enjoying an "excellent" teacher would also be 0.5 percent more likely to attend a university (Lowrey 2011, January 6, A14).

Nothing misleads like statistics[2] (and those who cite them), so more surprising than these economists' fantastical "findings" were the straight faces with which they were reported. How could anyone possibly know it had been *teachers* who were responsible for the increased test scores? How did they know it had not been the *parents*? How about the live-in grandmother who helped with homework? (Never mind that the very concept of "influence" is too subtle and temporally complex to be quantified.) How did the economists know that those test scores did not rise due to vitamins or daily exercise or the well-lighted desk where the student was able to study without interruption? And surely the devout will want some credit kept for God. What about "effort" on the student's part? Is there no credit to be accorded to the kid who took the test? How does the apparently increasing incidence of cheating on these tests figure in?[3]

Economics is specifically unsuited to the study of education. For starters, its conception of the human subject—as a self-interested rational individual (see Coyle 2007, 5, 124, 144)—is simplistic. "For if

DOI: 10.1057/9781137303424

economics accepted without question the psychic diversity of motivation," Steve Fuller (1993, 142) points out, "then the quantitative basis of the discipline would be undermined, given that values cannot be calculated unless they are reducible to a common currency of utilities." Reductionism is not the only problem for the field of economics; so is its tendency to substitute correlation for causality. In historical studies, Diane Coyle admits, no reciprocal relation between education and economic growth has ever been found: "Yet education cannot have been decisive during the Industrial Revolution, when literacy levels were low, and many innovators hadn't been to school at all" (Coyle 2007, 51). Perhaps today, with education reduced to job preparation, a closer correlation is conceivable (see Coyle 2007, 50), but confusing correlation with causation, as Chetty, Friedman, and Rockoff have done, cannot advance that cause, however misguided a cause reducing education to job preparation is.

The Chetty, Friedman, Rockoff research is also contradicted by the research of other economists who have shown that income, more than race or *any other factor*, is correlated with achievement quantified as test scores. The correlation between economic advantage and student performance has been documented for decades, notably by the famous Coleman Report in 1966. Recent research by Sean F. Reardon of Stanford University examined the achievement gap between children from high- and low-income families during the past 50 years. Reardon found that the difference in achievement between white and black students has "narrowed significantly" (Tavernise 2012, February 10, A1) over the past few decades, while the difference between rich and poor students has "grown substantially" during the same period (Tavernise 2012, February 10, A3). "We have moved from a society in the 1950s and 1960s, in which race was more consequential than family income, to one today in which family income appears more determinative of educational success than race," concludes Reardon (quoted in Tavernise 2012, February 10, A3). Reardon has found that the difference in standardized test scores between affluent and low-income students has increased by approximately 40 percent since the 1960s. It is now double the testing gap between blacks and whites. The correlation of income inequality[4] with educational accomplishment was underscored in another study, this one conducted by researchers at the University of Michigan. They found that the difference between rich and poor children in college completion—statistically the single most important predictor of success in the work

DOI: 10.1057/9781137303424

force—had increased by about 50 percent since the late 1980s (Tavernise 2012, February 10, A3).[5]

As have teachers for a century, Helen Ladd and Edward Fiske (2011, December 12, A21) asked: "Can anyone credibly believe that the mediocre overall performance of American students on international tests is unrelated to the fact that one-fifth of American children live in poverty?" While poverty is not to be recommended, recall that this data is correlational. Besides poverty, cultural and familial as well as individual and psychological characteristics are no doubt determinative. Poverty is to be opposed because it is immoral, not only because those children who suffer it will score lower on standardized tests. On that point Ladd and Fiske concur.

Not since President Lyndon Baines Johnson's *War on Poverty* has the elimination of poverty in the United States been a viable political issue. Since school reformers decline to tackle poverty, they provide forms of social support and experiences that middle-class students evidently enjoy as a matter of course. Ladd and Fiske (2011, December 12, A21) cite the Harlem Children's Zone (there are problems there: see Pinar 2012, 28, 203), the East Durham, North Carolina Children's Initiative, and Say Yes to Education in Syracuse, N.Y. I would add a 1980s example—LSYOU at Louisiana State University—where underachieving, poor, mostly black kids were housed on the LSU campus during the summer and provided intensive academic tutoring and social counseling. These programs are important as moral efforts at reparation, not as exemplars of social engineering.

The average SAT score of students from families earning more than $100,000 per year is more than 100 points higher than for students in the income rage of $50,000 to $60,000. Given these figures it is inevitable that only 3 percent of students in the most highly ranked 150 colleges and universities in the US come from families in the bottom income quartile of American society. As Andrew Delbanco (2012, March 9, A21) point outs, "students from affluent families have many advantages—test-prep tutors, high schools with good college counseling, parents with college savvy and so on." Rather than measuring aptitude for academic success, college-entrance examinations are retrospective reflections of family income, enabling the monied to leverage economic into academic advantage.

The culture of competition—not of contemplation—intensifies, reaching back from secondary school into early- and middle-childhood

DOI: 10.1057/9781137303424

education. In New York City, for instance, competition for admission to academically respected middle schools has become acute. Students' scores on fourth- and fifth-grade standardized tests is one prerequisite to admission. Many parents—some wealthy, some not—are now spending hundreds and thousands of dollars for tutors and for courses. Never mind that almost all elementary schools now provide their own test preparation anyway (Phillips 2012, April 16, A14).

The Education Department has not discouraged private tutoring, nor would officials even comment when asked if they are concerned that private tutoring afforded wealthier students an unfair advantage in middle-school admissions. Evidently tutoring *does* provide such as advantage, as the Department has already noted an unusual rise in high scores on its tests for gifted programs, administered to 4- and 5-year-olds. High scores on these exams do not guarantee admission, however. They simply qualify the student to take yet another test, this one administered by the school itself (Phillips 2012, April 16, A14–A15). Constant testing replaces academic study, installing ignorance not erudition as outcomes.

A researcher at the Center for Advanced Studies at the Juan March Institute in Madrid, Sabino Kornrich, and a sociologist at the University of Pennsylvania, Frank F. Furstenberg, found that in 1972 affluent Americans were spending *five* times as much per child on education as low-income families. But by 2007 that difference in expenditure had increased to *nine* to one, as spending by upper-income families has more than doubled, while spending by low-income families increased by only 20 percent. "The pattern of privileged families today is intensive cultivation," observed Furstenberg (quoted in Tavernise 2012, February 10, A3).

In addition to tutors and test prep, what does affluence buy? It appears "time" and "experiences" are also among what can be purchased. An economist at the University of Chicago, James J. Heckman, argues that parenting matters as much as, if not more than, income in forming a child's cognitive ability and personality during the pre-school years. An associate professor of public policy and sociology at the UCLA, Meredith Phillips, used survey data to show that affluent children spend 1,300 more hours than low-income children before age 6 in places other than their homes, e.g. their day care centers, or schools, from museums to shopping malls. By the time high-income children start school, they have enjoyed approximately 400 hours more than poor children in literary activities, Phillips found (Tavernise 2012, February 10, A3).

DOI: 10.1057/9781137303424

Like the conclusions of the survey research Meredith Phillips reported, geophysicist David Deming underscores the educational experience children enjoy at home as crucial to their later learning. He cites "reading" as primary, but he also worries about what "teachers can do with children who have not been challenged at home but instead have been indulged and entertained with an array of electronic devices" (Deming 2012, February 1, A15). Deming (2012, February 1, A15) is emphatic on this point: "Video-games have no educational value whatsoever. They are degrading, addictive, and stultifying." He recommends books; they are "infinitely more beneficial" than "any type of electronic device." Given the deluge of endorsements[6] of "gaming" as supportive of cognitive development, that is brave advice.

Questions of the quality of childhood and the effects of economic inequality disappear in the contemporary obsession with test scores. It is unsurprising that curriculum studies in the United States is contracting in an era dominated by numbers. Those most qualified to understand what is at stake in educating the public for democracy—curriculum studies specialists—are being replaced with economists who correlate data but who are not trained (evidently) to distinguish between correlation and causality, let alone to ask the crucial curriculum question: *what knowledge is of most worth?* In this economistic era—in which the state of the economy, not the state of society or spirituality or sustainability, is the main thing—it is to be expected that economists enjoy an inflated influence. But even some economists have become alarmed at the moral corruption such power tempts.

At their January 2012 national meeting, US economists adopted new rules requiring them to disclose their financial ties to companies and to other groups that consult them. Critics both inside and outside the profession have alleged that those relationships—often lucrative and undisclosed—have influenced economists' work negatively, so that, for instance, most economists missed the signs of the impending financial disaster of 2008. (So much for evidence-based research![7]) More specifically, it is clear that many economists make policy recommendations that are in their *clients'* interests, not in the interests of the economy overall (Casselman 2012, January 9, A2). (There was not one reference in the report to the *public* interest.) The new rules of professional conduct that US economists adopted will make more transparent their role in policymaking, presumably reducing the incidence of moral corruption. Do the economists referenced earlier—Chetty, Friedman, and Rockoff—have

DOI: 10.1057/9781137303424

financial investments in the test-making industry? If so, these will now be disclosed, presumably. How one wishes the moral corruption decoyed by the concept "school reform"—with its scapegoating of teachers and exploitation of children by computer companies[8]—would be become transparent to the American public.

Race to the top

Although the Obama administration still promotes its *Race to the Top* initiative, it disavows its programmatic progenitor: George W. Bush's *No Child Left Behind*. Secretary of Education Arne Duncan told Congress in 2011 that *NCLB* would result in condemning 82 percent of all the nation's public schools as failing. Skeptics questioned that projection, but Duncan insisted on its accuracy; President Obama repeated it in a speech three days later (Dillon 2011, December 15, A28). After having adopted the worst features of *No Child Left Behind* with its school-as-a-business model, by 2012 the Obama administration was dissociating itself from the political embarrassment created by failing to meet those "profit projections" (e.g. standardized test score results) it had adopted from *NCLB*.

In late 2011, a new study made clear that the administration's statistics—that under NCLB criteria 82 percent of all US schools were failing—were mistaken. The study, by the Center on Education Policy, a Washington research group led by a Democratic lawyer who had endorsed most of the administration's education policies, reported that 48—not 82—percent of the nation's schools would have been labeled as failing under *NCLB*. Duncan dismissed the discrepancy: "Whether it's 50 percent or 80 percent of schools being incorrectly labeled as failing, one thing is clear: *No Child Left Behind* is broken." (Dillon 2011, December 15, A28). Trying to wiggle out of a political problem predestined by *NCLB* and *Race to the Top*, Duncan lacks the insight and integrity to acknowledge the fundamental error that is "school reform."

By July 2012 the Obama administration had freed 31 states and the District of Columbia from its crucial provisions, including the deadline for bringing all students to "proficiency" in reading and mathematics by 2014 (Rich 2012, July 27, A14). While maintaining that the goals of the *No Child* law were the right ones, Obama added: "we've got to do it in a way that doesn't force teachers to teach to the test, or encourage

DOI: 10.1057/9781137303424

schools to lower their standards to avoid being labeled as failures" (Hu 2012, February 10, A13).⁹ Logic has never been related to school "reform," a manufactured crisis (see Berliner and Biddle 1995) aimed at displacing responsibility for the state of the nation from politicians to school teachers (Pinar 2012, 104).

Scapegoating teachers has been the key tactic in keeping the "crisis" rhetoric alive. Like many other Democrats, Washington state Governor Chris Gregoire has colluded with the right-wing's misrepresentation of the profession: "We need to address this concern out there that we have bad teachers," Gregoire said (quoted in La Corte 2011, December 14, A9). Note that she is not asserting there are "bad teachers...out there," but the Governor felt compelled to be responsive to even libelous allegations, converting them, in her statement, to "concern." While claiming schools fail to produce eligible candidates for jobs, corporate leaders salivate at the sight of unprotected public budgets, ripe for pillaging, theft conducted in the name of school "reform" (see Spring 2012).

If there is ever a Nuremburg-style trial over these crimes against humanity—specifically against schoolchildren, but also against the teachers who labor to educate them—Gregoire will be charged as one of many "collaborators," e.g. yet another politician who has capitulated to corporations plundering public budgets. When asked by reporters if school reform was required in order to obtain the political support for a sales tax increase of locally based corporations such as Microsoft and Boeing, Gregoire insisted it was no "quid pro quo." "These two employers desperately need a skilled workforce," she offered. "They made that very clear to me" (quoted in La Corte 2011, December 14, A9), once again playing the shell game of dissimulation.

Where is the irony when business leaders demand that schools comply with their demands to train future employees? Never mind their ignorance of the purpose of public education in a democracy. Even on business grounds alone one would think Bill Gates and his cronies would exercise some restraint, given their bungling of specific businesses (including, on occasion, Microsoft) and, most importantly, of the overall economy, most dramatically in 2008, but during the recovery as well, as corporations keep billions of profits overseas, safe from US taxation. Instead of restraint there is the pretense of professional competence and public authority. Microsoft General Counsel and Executive Vice President Brad Smith announced that he was "encouraged by Governor Gregoire's willingness to propose necessary improvements to our

DOI: 10.1057/9781137303424

education system, and we view her proposals today as a positive step in the right direction" (quoted in La Corte 2011, December 14, A9). As it has in specific businesses and as it threatened to do in 2008 to the world economy, corporate arrogance can only destroy public education in the United States.[10]

The end of public education in the United States

With Bill Gates and his foundation playing major roles in dismantling public education in America, can anyone be surprised it is being accomplished by replacing schools with online instruction, the infrastructure of which will be provided by key computer corporations such as Microsoft?[11] By late 2011 numerous states and school districts across the United States were establishing online public schools that allow students from kindergarten to twelfth grade to take some—or all—of their classes from anywhere other than actual schools. Consistent with the National Education Technology Plan, even those students still attending schools are being forced to undergo instruction that is largely computer-based and self-directed (see Spring 2012, 59–69).

Estimates range from just under 200,000 (Saul 2011, December 13, A1) to 250,000 (Banchero and Simon 2011, November 12) children now enrolled in full-time virtual schools, up 40 percent in the past three years. More than two million pupils take at least one class online, according to the International Association for K12 Online Learning, a trade group. Banchero and Simon (2011, November 12–13, C1) report that while some states and local districts operate their own online schools, many others hire for-profit corporations such as K12 Inc. of Herndon, Va., and Connections Academy in Baltimore, a subsidiary of the technology company Pearson PLC. These companies—not school-district selected professional educators—hire teachers, provide curriculum, monitor student performance as they lobby to promote online education. No longer public services, curriculum and teaching are now products sold to the public, substituting corporate profitability for professional commitment to children's education.[12]

By almost every quantitative measure, Saul (2011, December 13, A1) reports, the Agora Cyber Charter School is a failure. Some 60 percent of its students fall below grade level in math and almost 50 percent trail in reading. A third of its students fail to graduate on time, and

DOI: 10.1057/9781137303424

hundreds of children, from kindergartners to seniors, withdraw within months after they enroll. By Wall Street standards—profitability, not professional commitment to educate children—Agora is a striking success that has helped enrich K12 Inc., the publicly traded company that manages the school. The entire enterprise is paid for by taxpayers. "Kids mean money," Saul (2011, December 13, A1) reports. In "school reform" children are not pupils but numbers: profits, commodities to be bought and sold.

Agora anticipates income of $72 million this school year, accounting for more than 10 percent of the total anticipated revenues of K12. It is the major player in the online-school business. The second largest—Connections Education—was bought this year by the publishing corporation Pearson for $400 million. K12 Inc. aggressively circulates school reformers' assertions that corporate efficiencies combined with the internet can revolutionize public education, offering high quality at reduced cost. Surprisingly—given its history of uncritical, even colluding, editorial statements on school reform in recent years—*The New York Times* investigated K12 Inc. Through interviews and reviews of school finances and performance records, the *Times'* investigation "raises serious questions" about whether K12 schools (and full-time online schools generally) "benefit children or taxpayers," especially as state education budgets are being "slashed" (Saul 2011, December 13, A1). What the *Times* found was a company that produces profits (plundering public-school budgets) by increasing enrollment, increasing teacher workload, and lowering standards (Saul 2011, December 13, A18).

Current and former staff members of K12 Inc. schools report that employees are directed to conduct "intense" recruitment campaigns that admit students who are unlikely to succeed. Online education requires parental commitment and self-propelled students. Saul somehow fails to mention that if "brick-and-mortar" schools could also enlist strong parental involvement and self-motivated students, there would be fewer statistics that could be used to support relocating curriculum online. Given that students are unprepared for what K12 Inc. offers, programs are adjusted by "reducing curriculum and teachers" (Saul 2011, December 13, A18). Despite lower operating costs, the online companies cost nearly as much as public schools, except that all funds are not going to curriculum and instruction but to personal profits and the inflated salaries of corporate "entrepreneurs."

DOI: 10.1057/9781137303424

These facts erase any rationale for school reform. When faced with the facts of their own failure, company spokesmen either question the legitimacy of test results or blame the public schools. The chief executive of K12 Inc., Ronald J. Packard, admitted there had been "degradation" in K12's test scores, but he insisted that these scores were an unreliable measure given that many students are "already behind" when they commence the program (quoted in Saul 2011, December 13, A18). He failed to note that many students are just as "behind" when they arrive at regular schools, a long-term rationale for Head-Start and other preparatory programs. Never mind that the very concept of "behind" is a product of standardized scores that are entirely self-referential, not reflective of students' actual educational achievement (Pinar 2012, xii). What is obvious here is that this corporate spokesman has no professional commitment to education; what he has is a well-paying job he will say anything to protect.

Instead of truth telling we are subjected to yet another example of scapegoating, the long-time strategy of school reformers (Pinar 2012, 104). Packard insisted that *the failure of K12 is entirely the public schools' fault.* "Kids have been shackled to their brick-and-mortar school down the block for too long," he said repeatedly, adding that parents, for the first time he thought, have choices where they enroll their children in school. (Never mind that Catholic and other religious and private schools have offered parents "choices" for two centuries in the United States.) "It's a choice," allowed Thomas L. Seidenberger, superintendent of the East Penn School District in Pennsylvania, in response to this story. He added: "What about a bad choice?" His public-school district is "outperforming" Agora[13] and other online schools its students attend (Saul 2011, December 13, A18). If school reform had ever been about facts, public funds would now be reallocated away from K12 and to the East Penn School District.

Much as military contractors profit from Pentagon spending, Saul (2011, December 13, A18) points out, school reformers—like the infamous Michael R. Milken, whose company Knowledge Universe started K12 a decade ago and who remains an investor—exploit public education as a source of government-financed profits. To increase profits, a "sizable portion" of the public funds collected by K12 is spent not on instruction but on generating new business, a common business practice that nevertheless raises ethical questions. After all, these public funds were allocated to educate schoolchildren, not line the pockets of profiteers.

DOI: 10.1057/9781137303424

K12 spent $26.5 million on advertising in 2010 (Saul 2011, December 13, A18).

Parents who are considering enrolling their children in K12's schools can call 866 numbers, which connect them to a call center. School personnel who have visited the center have reported that it is a "high-pressure sales environment" structured by one objective: increased enrollment. Like those in the finance industry who were paid according to the number of mortgages refinanced (however deceptive the terms), K12 "enrollment pals" are also rewarded with bonuses according to the number of students they sign up. Packard's annual bonus is also partly tied to enrollment, Saul (2011, December 13, A18) confirms. Record-keeping becomes less rigorous once students are enrolled, as a state audit of the Colorado Virtual Academy revealed. There, public funds had paid for students who were not students at the school. The state of Colorado ordered reimbursement of more than $800,000. With retention an ongoing issue, K12 teachers admit they were under pressure to pass students with marginal performance and attendance. Students only needed to log in to be marked present for the day, reported Agora teachers and administrators (Saul 2011, December 13, A18).

Rather than providing a public service, K12 Inc. exploits a market: the company estimates the market for its schools could be as high as $15 billion.[14] To capitalize on this potential, the company plans to expand across the United States. A recently acquired site of plundered public funds is Tennessee, where the company received legislative approval last May. In July it began holding information sessions, and by fall 1800 students had enrolled in the Tennessee Virtual Academy. In Pennsylvania, where K12 Inc. collects about 10 percent of its revenues, the company has spent $681,000 on lobbying since 2007 while contributing—according to National Institute on Money in State Politics—almost $500,000 to state political candidates across the country from 2004 to 2010 (Saul 2011, December 13, A19).

Stanford University's Center for Research on Education Outcomes studied students in eight virtual schools in Pennsylvania, including Agora, comparing them with similar students in regular schools. The study found that "in every subgroup, with significant effects, *cyber charter performance is lower*" (quoted in Saul 2011, December 13, A19, emphasis added). Has "business" become in the United States the new church, somehow exempt from public criticism? Once a public trust held sacred for children's futures, schools are now the targets of corporations who

DOI: 10.1057/9781137303424

fail to protect not only the public but in 2008 even their own economic viability. Opportunists exploit for profit the American public's amnesia.

Playing *exactly* the same scapegoating card that politicians had used after the 1957 Sputnik satellite launching (Pinar 2012, 102–104) and again in the early 1980s—then with the 1983 publication of *A Nation at Risk* (National Commission on Excellence in Education. 1983; Pinar 2012, 200–202)—former Secretary of State Condoleezza Rice and the former chancellor of New York City's schools, Joel I. Klein[15] warned in March 2012 that the nation's security and economic prosperity are at risk if schools fail to improve. "The dominant power of the 21st century will depend on human capital," repeated the report by a panel the two discredited figures headed up. "The failure to produce that capital will undermine American security" (quoted passages in Associated Press 2012, March 20, A12). Few have threatened US homeland security and economic stability more than the administration of George W. Bush, in which Rice was a key player. Few have done more to destroy public education than Klein (see Pinar 2012, 22–23). Fear worked well politically for the George W. Bush administration, a lesson evidently not lost on either Rice or Klein.

Never mind the truth, there's money to be made. Not only the education of children is being sacrificed by K12 Inc. and other corporations posing as "schools," children's overall psychological well-being is apparently at risk as well when too much time is spent online. Researchers from Stanford University surveyed 3,461 girls from the ages of 8 to 12 regarding their use of electronic devices and the state of their social and emotional lives. They found that frequent digital multitasking and extensive time spent in front of screens correlated with poor emotional and social health, indicators of which included low social confidence, feeling abnormal, sleeplessness and having more friends whom parents considered as poor influences. Watching videos, online or on television, was in particular strongly associated with troubled social and emotional development (Silverman 2012, January 31, D2).

Media multitasking may have "serious emotional and developmental consequences," said Clifford Nass, a communications professor at Stanford and co-author of the study with Roy Pea, an education professor (quoted in Silverman 2012, January 31, D2). While they found a strong correlation between heavy media multitasking and poor emotional health, Nass acknowledged that they had not been able to demonstrate causality. Nor were they able to specify an optimal amount of "face time"

DOI: 10.1057/9781137303424

or just how much digital multitasking was too much (Silverman 2012, January 31, D2).

Researchers reported the girls they studied spent an average of 6.9 hours a day using electronic media, versus 2.1 hours a day in "face-to-face interaction." Those girls who engaged in "high levels of face-to-face communication"—perhaps forms of orality?[16]—exhibited "strong" social and emotional health even if they were "heavy" media users (quoted passages in Silverman 2012, January 31, D2). The researchers speculated that children learn to read emotions by observing the faces of other people. That capability then enables them to feel more capable socially. The researchers also speculated that video-chatting—for instance over Skype—may be an "imperfect substitute" for "in-person conversations," in part due to the widespread practice of multitasking that diverts attention away from listening. Nass also said that when children are in the company of peers and family members who are themselves staring at screens, they also are less likely to be engaged emotionally:

> You used to hear all the time "Look at me when I talk to you," but now everyone is looking at their devices instead. I may hear the words you are using, but I miss the tone of your voice, your facial expressions and your body posture, so I get less facile with reading emotions. The most important message is that face-to-face communications is just enormously important and there has been a dramatic decline in that, among kids and among families. (quoted in Silverman 2012, January 31, D2).

Can moving the curriculum online do anything but exacerbate these outcomes?

With public budgets plundered by private corporations, what do children and teachers face in the schools that remain? In Texas, for instance, budget cuts not only removed teachers from classrooms, they required those remaining to take on additional, including non-professional, tasks. Parents are billed for services that were once provided as public services. In Forth Worth, in the Keller Independent School District, parents are now charged from $185 to $355 for one student for bus service to school. The district had already eliminated 100 positions and sports teams and was no longer able to provide security in schools, as budget cuts forced cancellation of contracts with local police agencies (Fernandez 2012, April 9, A10). In another Texas district, Dripping Springs, teachers were forced to do the work of the laid-off custodial staff. At Hutto High School, Eric Soto, a world history teacher and also the head softball coach and

DOI: 10.1057/9781137303424

assistant volleyball coach, no longer taught four classes. Forced to add a fifth class, Soto worked 12 to 20 more hours per week, both in classrooms and after school with the school's sports teams, even though his athletic bonus had been cut by about $2,000. District teachers have not received a raise in two years (Fernandez 2012, April 9, A10). Has the chief executive of K12 Inc., Ronald J. Packard, shared in the sacrifice?

Model schools?

Now many of us have known for decades that the educational potential of technology is fundamentally a matter of faith (Pinar and Grumet 2006 [1976]). Even Apple's co-founder Steve Jobs expressed skepticism that technology could improve education. In a conversation conducted in 2011, the dying Mr. Jobs and Bill Gates, the Microsoft co-founder, "agreed that computers had, so far, made surprisingly little impact on schools—far less than on other realms of society such as media and medicine and law" (quoted in Richtel 2011, November 5, B7). This admission echoed observations Mr. Jobs had expressed in 1996 in an interview with *Wired* magazine. Then Jobs had admitted that *"what's wrong with education cannot be fixed with technology"* (quoted Richtel 2011, November 5, B7, italics added). Despite this admission, Apple proceeded, proceeds still, with aggressive plans to exploit school budgets. It can't hurt having a former Apple executive—Karen Cator—as director of educational technology for the U. S. Department of Education (Schwarz 2012, February 13, A10).

Visiting educators from across the nation have roamed the halls and entered the classrooms of East Mooresville Intermediate School in North Carolina.[17] They search for the "secret formula." In Erin Holsinger's fifth-grade math class they thought they found it. There, a boy peering into his school-issued MacBook moved through fractions by himself, determined to reach the sixth-grade level by winter. Three desks away, a girl struggled with basic multiplication—her calculations were only 29 percent correct, the screen said—and Ms. Holsinger knelt beside her to help. "Curiosity was fed and embarrassment avoided," Schwarz (2012, February 13, A10) concluded, "as teacher connected with student through emotion far more than [had] Wi-Fi."

"This is not about the technology," Mark Edwards, superintendent of Mooresville Graded School District, explained to visitors later over lunch. "It's not about the box. It's about changing the culture of instruction—preparing students for their future, not our past" (quoted in Schwarz 2012, February 13, A10). Had Edwards had more respect for the past, he might have exhibited a more guarded enthusiasm, as technology has consistently failed to improve learning, and changing the "culture of instruction" is a meaningless mantra echoing through the twentieth century of educational reform. Its gendered and racial subtexts make clear its non-educational intents and catastrophic consequences (Pinar 2012, 132).

Edwards' ignorance appeals to the Obama administration. In September 2011, Edwards spoke on a White House panel; federal Department of Education officials often cite Mooresville as a great success. "Other districts are doing things, but what we see in Mooresville is the whole package: using the budget, innovating, using data, involvement with the community and leadership," pontificated Karen Cator, a former Apple executive who is (as noted earlier) the director of educational technology for the United States Department of Education. "There are lessons to be learned," she surmised (quoted passages in Schwarz 2012, February 13, A10). One lesson could have been learned from her great grandmother: keep the fox out of the henhouse.

Too late, as Apple has already plundered Mooresville's public budget. Each student's MacBook Air was leased from Apple for $215 a year, including warranty, for a total of $1 million; an additional $100,000 a year was allocated for software. Terry Haas, the district's chief financial officer, admitted the funds were freed up through "incredibly tough decisions" (quoted in Schwarz 2012, February 13, A10). Sixty-five jobs were eliminated, including 37 teaching positions, which resulted in larger class sizes—in middle schools it increased to 30 from 18—but district officials insisted that instruction was now more efficient due to the technology.[18] Not only public but private budgets suffer; Mooresville families now pay $50 a year to subsidize computer repairs, though the fee is waived for those who cannot afford it, almost 20 percent of parents. Similarly, the district has negotiated a deal so that those without broadband internet access can purchase it for $9.99 a month (Schwarz 2012, February 13, A10).

Laptops now perform the same tasks as those performed by teachers in hundreds of other districts, Schwarz (2012, February 13, A12) reports. They correct worksheets, organize so-called progress data, present

DOI: 10.1057/9781137303424

multimedia lessons while students work at their own pace or in groups. (Obviously Schwartz has only the most rudimentary idea of what teachers do.) The difference technology makes is that kids stare at screens rather than listening to teachers and to each other. Despite the demotion, Mooresville teachers and administrators were evidently enthusiastic, praising computers for presenting the "newest content" and for tapping the oldest of student emotions—curiosity, boredom, embarrassment, angst—leaving to educators to provide what only human beings can. What would that be?

In the example the *New York Times* reporter provided (see Schwarz 2012, February 13, A12), what human beings provide is prosthetic extensions of Google's software. Rather than explain Transcendentalism to her 11th-grade English students, the teacher—Katheryn Higgins—directed students to search Google Docs. That's all we're told. Did discussion follow? Was Ms. Higgins able to answer questions? Raise questions? On another occasion Higgins asked the more outgoing students to make presentations on the Declaration of Independence, while she encouraged the timid ones to speak about it in an online chat room (which Higgins monitored). There is no mention of the intellectual quality of the presentations or of students' understanding of anything.[19] Or that answering these questions underscores the importance of the individual teacher's judgment, a professional judgment informed by academic knowledge, and expressed as attuned to a particular situation. Instead, the report focuses exclusively on "behavior" and "organization," those two quintessentially American concepts, concepts as simplistic as they have been destructive (Pinar 2011a, 77–91).

There was another image of classroom life revealed in this report on "school reform" in Mooresville, North Carolina. One fourth grader was instructed by the software to complete ten multiplication questions in two minutes. If she accomplished this objective, she would be permitted to move to the next assignment. The student achieved the objective, but the lesson learned would seem to be the one teachers in Atlanta learned last year: cheat when necessary (Schwarz 2011, August 8, A10). Schwarz (2012, February 13, A12) observed that this Mooresville student simply consulted her times tables for the answers the software demanded, making the exercise not one of mathematical calculation but of speed typing. Perhaps the student was inspired by the Apple logos in the hallways of her school, and by the district's unofficial slogan: "iBelieve, iCan, iWill."

DOI: 10.1057/9781137303424

Huxley's brave new world is here and now, and not only in Mooresville, North Carolina.

In 2011, the Idaho state legislature overwhelmingly passed a law requiring all high-school students to take online classes in order to graduate. As in North Carolina, the state promised to provide all students and their teachers laptops or tablets. To pay for these purchases, the state shifted tens of millions of dollars away from teacher salaries. State bureaucrats also announced a shift in the role of teachers, who, they announced, would no longer be "lecturers," standing at the front of classrooms. Now teachers would be "guides," their teaching focused only on helping students complete whatever lessons appeared on those computer screens (Richtel 2012, January 4, A1, B4).

In the spring of 2011 Idaho teachers marched on the state capital, protesting that their lawmakers had "listened less to them than to heavy lobbying by technology companies, specifically Intel and Apple" (quoted in Richtel 2012, January 4, B4). Teacher and parent groups gathered 75,000 verified signatures, more than was needed, for a referendum that could invalidate the legislation (Richtel 2012, January 4, B4). That vote will be taken in November 2012.

"This technology is being thrown on us. It's being thrown on parents and thrown on kids," complained Idaho high-school English teacher Ann Rosenbaum. Rosenbaum is no pawn of the powerful teacher unions,[20] as politicians and profiteers often portray those who criticize their schemes. Rather, Rosenbaum is a former military police officer in the US Marines Corp and a member of the Republican party (quoted passage in Richtel 2012, January 4, B4). Rather than relying on technology, Rosenbaum relies on conversation, engaging her students with her own (not scripted) questions. While technology has a role to play in classrooms she allows, Rosenbaum reminded the reporter observing her that her method of teaching—Socratic questioning—is timeless: "I'm teaching them to think deeply, to *think*. A computer can't do that" (quoted in Richtel 2012, January 4, B4). Idaho Governor C. L. Otter doesn't understand all the fuss, commenting that "putting technology into students' hands" is the "only way to prepare them for the workforce" (Richtel 2012, January 4, B4). Never mind that by the time students reach the workforce the technology will have changed. Never mind that public education is not job preparation.[21] Never mind that teachers' accomplishments cannot be quantified.

DOI: 10.1057/9781137303424

Teaching not testing

In February 2012, the New York City teacher data reports, covering three school years ending in 2010, were released. Presumably these show how much "value" individual teachers "add" by reporting how much their students' test scores exceeded expectations based on demographics and prior performance. Such "value-added assessments" are promoted by the Obama administration's *Race to the Top* initiative. New York City principals have made them a part of tenure decisions. They are increasingly being used in new teacher-evaluation systems across the nation. For instance, Houston schools gave bonuses based in part on value-added measures, and in Washington, poorly rated teachers lost their jobs. These assessments, Santos and Gebeloff (2012, February 25, A15) acknowledge, are an "imprecise science," citing that the margin of error for the math ratings in New York City was 35 percentiles, and for English 53 percentiles. Teachers were ranked on as few as ten students.

Despite being ranked highly, New York City teacher Alison Epstein said she declined to teach to the test, affirming instead her commitment to teach in a "fun, hands-on manner." To illustrate "comparing and contrasting," Epstein had asked students read an article describing a Pakistani girl's daily routine, then compose essays comparing their lives with hers (quoted passages in Hu and Gebeloff 2012, February 27, A15). Now teaching a second-grade gifted and talented class at P.S. 33 in the Chelsea neighborhood of Manhattan, Epstein criticized the ratings system in which she had excelled. She pointed out that there were too many variables to link test students' score results with teaching: for example, even students who enjoy supportive parents might suffer from a lack of focus on test day. "Unfortunately, the schools have become incredibly data-driven, which at times detracts from the overall curriculum," Epstein said. "The pressure for teachers and children to perform for tests that do not really show how intelligent a student is, or how amazing a teacher might be, is substantial" (quoted passages in Hu and Gebeloff 2012, February 27, A15).

Epstein is hardly alone. "I believe the teachers will be right in feeling assaulted and compromised here," Merryl H. Tisch, the chancellor of the State Board of Regents, admitted in an interview. "And I just think, from every perspective, it sets the wrong tone moving forward" (quoted in Santos and Gebeloff 2012, February 25, A15). As I have complained (Pinar 2012, 28), teachers' unions have failed to protect teachers from

DOI: 10.1057/9781137303424

being demonized, but perhaps this might change. In the days before the release of ratings for thousands of New York City public-school teachers, hundreds of emails poured into the inbox of Michael Mulgrew, president of the United Federation of Teachers. "Enough of cooperation," one member of the union wrote to Mulgrew. Others prodded Mulgrew to stand up against Mayor Michael R. Bloomberg, describing him as "untrustworthy." "What I'm going to do now," Mulgrew said in an interview over the weekend, "is to stop the mayor from doing any further damage to the children of New York City" (Santos and Phillips 2012, February 27, A13). Aggressive union action is past due.

In February 2012, officials of the Charlotte-Mecklenburg Schools shelved 52 end-of-the-year exams that had been devised to measure teacher effectiveness. The exams had been used for only one year before being discarded, victim not of teachers' intransigence but parents' outrage[22] at the very idea of kindergarten exams, even if administered one student at a time. The assessment took up too much instructional time, they pointed out (Banchero 2012, March 8, A2). Assessment of whatever ilk focuses instructional time on measurable outcomes, ignoring the more significant educational experiences that children can enjoy and from which they might learn but may show no signs of having learned for years to come.

Pamela Grundy, the mother of a fifth-grader and co-chairwoman of Mecklenburg Area Coming Together for Schools, a parent advocacy group, is convinced that parental protest had turned the tide. Grundy recalled that school-board meetings had been packed with parents who were "appalled" by the increase in student testing. "We thought it was stifling kids' creativity and warping our children's classroom experience," she told *The New York Times* reporter (quoted passages in Banchero 2012, March 8, A2.)

Memphis music teacher Jeff Chipman is working with other teachers in piloting the new assessment based on student portfolios, an assessment strategy long-standing in curriculum studies (Salvio 1998). "We are about teaching kids to perform and experience art, and that cannot be measured with a pencil-and-paper test," he said. "We want to be evaluated on how we help kids grow, but we don't want to turn the arts program into a testing machine" (quoted in Banchero 2012, March 8, A2).

However sound, teachers' professional judgment continues to be suspect, and uninformed legislators continue to intervene in what are properly professional matters. For instance, during 2012, lawmakers

DOI: 10.1057/9781137303424

in Colorado, New Mexico, Iowa, and Tennessee considered legislation that would force students to repeat third grade if they are unable to pass state reading exams. Such legislation has revived decades-long debates regarding the retention of students. Does it support student achievement or make more likely dropping out? Unsurprisingly, the evidence is mixed on whether retention helps or hurts (Banchero 2012, February 13, A3). Diane Ravitch (2000, 405) had blamed underachievement (yes, only defined by test scores) on a curricular "electivism" that had allowed US students to avoid more intellectually demanding courses and enroll instead in "easier alternatives."[23] Only teacher judgment could individualize retention decisions. Just as parents must decide what is best for their children—taking into account expert advice, knowledge of their children's history and tendencies as well as their own instincts—a teacher too can recommend whether or not, in a particular case, retention or promotion is educationally sensible.

The absurdity of accountability becomes blatant in its extremes. Consider the absurd lengths to which Muhammad Zaman, a Boston University biomedical engineering professor, goes. Every other Monday, just before class ends, Lewin (2012, March 29, A18) reports, Zaman distributes a one-page form asking students to anonymously rate him and the course on a scale of one to five. What do the numbers represent? Zaman asks: "How can the professor improve your learning of the material?" "Has he improved his teaching since the last evaluation? In particular, has he incorporated your suggestions?" "How can the material be altered to improve your understanding of the material?" "Anything else you would like to convey to the professor?" (quoted in Lewin 2012, March 29, A18). In a culture of narcissism, such invitations to make the class about "me" are bound to say more about the respondents than they do about Professor Zaman's teaching.

Indeed, students' responses range widely, Zaman acknowledges, and they include comments like "Nice shirts." Another student requested: "Can we watch wrestling at the end? Please?" Despite such narcissistic nonsense, Professor Zaman seems oblivious, insisting that such comments can help him teach. Zaman felt sure his first reading assignment was accessible, for instance, but several non-science students claimed that it was incomprehensible. That information did not persuade him to delete that assignment—"Students don't choose the curriculum," he reassured the reporter—but he did begin distributing a list of terms and definitions (quoted passage in Lewin 2012, March 29, A18). Such

DOI: 10.1057/9781137303424

a list could prove helpful, provided students consult it. Emphasizing the professor's obligation to help students learn is laudable, but it can create the illusion that the professor, not the student, is responsible for his or her learning. If there are indecipherable terms, one consults the dictionary and/or asks questions in class. Trying to anticipate students' every need—*wrestling* you say?—underscores their status as consumers[24] not students, an anti-intellectual, deeply anti-educational identity. What about the intellectual quality of what Zaman teaches? Does this constant rechecking of students' comments take time away from his research? How can he remain current—let alone participate—in the "cutting edge" of his field's research if he is considering whether or not to show wrestling videos?

Students, not teachers, are responsible for students' success or failure. Obviously teachers—and others, including parents, relatives, and friends—can help, but it is students who must—if they wish to learn—take advantage of the opportunities teachers offer them. This apparently incomprehensible fact was illustrated when the winners of 2012 *New York Times* College Scholarships were announced.[25] One student had spent her childhood in four homeless shelters, had been forced to attend 12 different schools, and during high school worked 20 hours a week at a supermarket so she could pay for her imprisoned father to call her regularly (collect). Another student did not see his father during the first 12 years of his life—except for webcam conversations—because he was living in China while his mother worked as an illegal immigrant in a New York City restaurant. A third winner of a scholarship was abandoned when her parents divorced and moved away; she moved in with her stepgrandfather. Despite these crushing circumstances, these three students excelled at their New York City high schools (Berger 2012, February 25, A16). Students can learn despite difficult circumstances.

Preying on public budgets, profiteers line their own pockets while schoolchildren stare at screens, curriculum structured like tax-returns that talk back. As corrupt as present circumstances are in the United States, they did not appear overnight. They developed over decades, and their causes are multiple. In very general terms we can blame the corporatization of society and the disappearance of the public sphere and its previous occupants, e.g. citizens, now converted to consumers. Yes, "power" is reproduced, but can Idaho English Teacher Ann Rosenbaum's fidelity to Socratic questioning be recoded as "resistance?" As a Republican and a former Marine, can we assume that she is a "critical

DOI: 10.1057/9781137303424

pedagogue?" Are our concepts adequate in understanding how it is that politicians and profiteers can pronounce Ann Rosenbaum's method of teaching—questioning—as irrelevant and out-of-date (see Richtel 2012, January 4, B4)? To ask that question requires us to engage in an intellectual history of the present.

Notes

1   Even apologists for economics admit that it fails in its primary purpose, as the field remains unable to explain, let alone predict, what accounts for economic growth. "[W]e're not entirely sure, or every economy would be growing," admits Diane Coyle (2007, 36). Others suggest that the "we" Coyle invokes to imply a disciplinary consensus is in fact a fabrication. "The existence and unity of a discipline called economics," Amariglio, Resnick, and Wolff (1993, 150) go so far to say, "reside in the eye and mind of the beholder." As is the case with other disciplines—curriculum studies is only one example—the discipline of economics is in fact an "agonistic" and "shifting" field of deeply different and often conflicting concepts in which there is little consensus concerning boundaries, objects or methods (1993, 150). What is clear is that, in David Harvey (2010, 28) summary: "In a desperate attempt to find more places to put the surplus capital, a vast wave of privatization swept around the world carried on the backs of the dogma that state-run enterprises are by definition inefficient and lax and that the only way to improve their performance is to pass them over the private sector." That "them" includes the public schools, as we see.

2   "For example," Andrew Feenberg (2010, 142) notes, "quantitative studies were long thought to 'prove' the irrelevance of classroom size to learning outcomes, contrary to the testimony of professional teachers. This 'proof' was very convenient for state legislators, anxious to cut budgets, but resulted in an educational disaster that, like the Challenger accident, could not be denied. Similar abuses of cost/benefit analysis are all to familiar."

3   The Associated Press characterized 2011 as "the year of the test cheating scandals." From Atlanta to Philadelphia and Washington to Los Angeles, hundreds of educators have been formally charged with changing answers on tests or providing answers to students. Evidently students are cheating when they can—not a recent development, of course—but the cases seem more spectacular: on Long Island, New York, for instance, at least 20 students were charged with cheating on SAT and ACT college-entrance exams by paying someone to take the test for them (Turner 2011, January 3, B5). "This problem existed before *No Child Left Behind* (NCLB), but NCLB

has exacerbated the problem, clearly," said Walter Haney, a retired Boston College education professor and expert on cheating (quoted in Turner 2011, January 3, B5). One of the darlings of school reform, Michelle Rhee (see Pinar 2012, 21–22), is now implicated in an investigation being conducted by the Office of the Inspector General in the US Department of Education. Officials are investigating whether Washington school officials cheated to raise test scores during Rhee's superintendency. "You would think," Michael Winerip (2012, February 27, A10) points out, that "Mr. Duncan [Secretary of the US Department of Education] would want to keep Ms. Rhee at arm's length during the investigation. And yet there they were, sitting side by side last month, two of four featured panelists at a conference in Washington on the use of education data." An investigator of the 2011 Atlanta testing scandal—identifying 178 teachers and principals in almost half of the Atlanta schools as cheating—Richard L. Hyde commented: "I'm shocked that the secretary of education would be fraternizing with someone who could potentially be the target of the investigation," he said. "The appearance of a conflict of interest is troubling because it can cause the public to lose faith in the investigation" (quoted in Winerip 2012, February 27, A10). The Atlanta and Washington situations are similar, Winerip points out, noting that both Michelle Rhee and Beverly Hall, the former Atlanta superintendent, both relied on fear to force their teachers to raise test scores. Like Rhee, Dr. Hall threatened that if scores didn't go up enough in three years, principals would be fired. Rhee bragged about how hard she pressed, Winerip reports: "We want educators to feel the pressure," she said (Winerip 2012, February 27, A10).

4 "Equality of opportunity," Peter Taubman (2009, 64–65) points out perceptively, "which would raise unsettling questions about resources, structures of privilege, and class and race, is replaced with equality of results, which of course is logically impossible.... Why? Because if everyone did well on the tests, then the cry would go up that the tests were too easy, reflected grade inflation, and revealed the 'dumbing down' of the curriculum, but if students fail, the cry goes up that the teachers are failing our students. It's a catch-22 that distracts from glaring inequalities of opportunity."

5 Tavernise (2012, February 10, A3) reports that these studies were concluded in 2007 and 2008, just before the Great Recession. Based on data from past recessions, the recent one is likely to have intensified the trend.

6 Suzanne De Castell and Jennifer Jenson (2003, 50) go so far as to suggest "gaming" and "play" as a "new paradigm" for curriculum research and development. "What we see in commercially produced computer games," they (2003, 50) explain, "is an extremely effective programming of learning opportunities which not only bypasses teaching but, more radically, bypasses linguistic articulation altogether." Game over, then, I'd say.

DOI: 10.1057/9781137303424

7 Even economics cannot claim "evidence" as basing its conclusions. Summarizing decades of economic research on questions of economic growth, Coyle (2007, 37) forefronts history and "luck" in understanding the phenomenon: "Rather, getting an economy expanding in the way the rich countries already have for the past 200 years depends on a complex sequence of decision and policies, involving many partners and depending on past choices, current resources, and pure luck."

8 "In most urban schools I visit," Dennis Carlson (2010, 204) reports, "the computer is still being used to program students, lead them down predictable paths, and produce standardized learning outcomes. And among middle-class cyborg youth, the possibilities opened up by the new technologies are largely wasted on idle chatter and mind-numbing games."

9 Despite the Obama admission of the failure of NCLB, as a face-saving gesture the Administration still insists that school districts reward "high-performing" schools and identify "low-performing" schools for "intervention," formulating "plans for improving educational outcomes for poor and minority students, non-native English speakers, students with disabilities, and other underperforming groups" (Hu 2012, February 10, A13).

10 "To fully grasp the irony of the assumption that CEOs...are the best ones to run schools and determine educational policy," Peter Taubman (2009, 99, emphasis added) points out, "one need only consider the record of corporate malfeasance, economic upheavals, over-inflated markets, the horrifying effects of corporate policies on the environment, on poverty, on the gap between rich and poor, and on public life over the last twenty-five years, that is since 1983, the year *A Nation at Risk* appeared. *One would think educators would want to keep anyone connected to the business world as far away as possible from educational policy*, although clearly there is a place for salesmen and merchants and accountants and lawyers in the ancillary operations. Instead educators seem to fall over themselves to base education on the corporate model: witness, for example, the plea of Arthur Levine, the ex-president of Teachers' College, that school leadership programs be based on business models." While there are too many collaborators—like Levine—there are many more politicians and profiteers networked to "leverage" their influence. Joel Spring (2012, 122, 154 ff.) has provided a detailed map of these interlocking networks.

11 Gates and Microsoft are not alone, as Andrew Feenberg's (2010, 154) summary makes clear: "In the late 1990s, corporate strategists, state legislators, top university administrators, and 'futurologists' lined up behind a vision of online education based on automation and deskilling. Their goal was to replace (at least for the masses) face-to-face teaching by professional faculty with an industrial product, infinitely reproducible at decreasing unit cost, like CDs, videodiscs, or software. The overhead of education

would decline sharply, and the education 'business' would finally become profitable." See Spring 2012, 34–39.

12   The privatization of K12 public education in the US follows the privatization of higher education. Currently, students at for-profit colleges comprise 13 percent of the nation's college enrolment. The majority leaves without a degree (half of those within four months), and they account for disproportionate percent of defaults on student loans. For this "accomplishment" US taxpayers spent $32 billion in 2011 alone. During summer 2012 the US Senate Health, Education, Labor and Pensions Committee issued a report on its two-year investigation of the industry. "In this report, you will find overwhelming documentation of exorbitant tuition, aggressive recruiting practices, abysmal student outcomes, taxpayer dollars spent on marketing and pocketed as profit, and regulatory evasion and manipulation," reported Senator Thomas Harkin, chairman of the US Senate Health, Education, Labor and Pensions Committee. "These practices are not the exception—they are the norm. They are systemic throughout the industry, with very few individual exceptions" (quoted passages in Lewin 2012, July 30, A12). Of course profiteers demand the privatization K12 public education!

13   One suspects that parents will not be blamed for Agora's failures, despite the fact that parents, recast as "learning coaches," do much of the teaching (quoted phrase in Saul 2011, December 13, A18).

14   "Perhaps the two most pro-business administrations in the last seventy-five years have been the Ronald Reagan and George W. Bush administrations," Peter Taubman (2009, 103, emphasis added) reminds, "yet the former came into power wanting to dismantle the Department of Education and the latter expanded its powers, successfully use it to *open up education to the business community*. What changed was the awareness that *education was a new market*, one worth billions of dollars." Under Obama, billions of taxpayer funds have been squandered to encourage the conversion of public education from public trust to a profitable market. As a public trust education is not a commodity to be bought and sold.

15   Given his record as chancellor, can anyone be surprised that Klein is "one of Rupert Murdoch's closest advisers dealing with the British phone hacking scandal" (Chozick 2012, July 24, B3)? The Murdoch's media empire—the News Corporation—announced in late July 2012 that Klein will head up its education division.

16   Even economists like Diane Coyle (2007, 56) appear to acknowledge the importance of subjective presence in communication: "To spell it out, knowledge spillovers are made possible by the physical proximity of people, especially when it comes to sharing and exchange of complicated and abstract ideas, whether in software or a service such as finance or medicine.

DOI: 10.1057/9781137303424

This is why business executives still fly thousands of miles for face-to-face meetings, why universities exist, and why computer experts cluster gather in Silicon Valley. Human capital spillovers (positive or negative) are similarly amplified by the near presence of others." This would seem to be an argument against moving all education online. See Pinar 2011a, 210, n. 23.

17 A "modest" community located 20 miles north of Charlotte, Mooresville had been best known as home to several Nascar teams and drivers, Schwarz (2012, February 13, A10) reports, but in recent years it has emerged as "the de facto national model of the digital school." While Mooresville ranks only 100th out of 115 districts in North Carolina in terms of dollars spent per student—$7,415.89 a year—it is now third in test scores and second in graduation rates. Neither statistic tells us anything important, however, as test scores cannot measure learning and the rate of graduation may only indicate grade inflation.

18 The 2009–2010 layoffs—about 10 percent of the district's teachers—not only shifted funds from human beings to machines, it sent an unmistakable message to those teachers who remained. The layoffs, Mr. Edwards told the reporter, "helped weed out the most reluctant." And those who remained? Mr. Edwards told the reporter that he was able to persuade those that the technology would actually allow for "more personal" and "enjoyable interaction with students" (Schwarz 2012, February 13, A12). Coercion can be persuasive.

19 "So," Ms. Higgins asked her English class after the bell rang, "you think you're going to like transcendentalism?" [sic] "Only if you're a nonconformist," a student replied (quoted in Schwarz 2012, February 13, A12). Not an adequate answer or a particularly precise question, but what does ring clear is that this school produces conformity, and not just social conformity, but intellectual conformity.

20 Those who scapegoat teachers scapegoat their unions—the Bill & Melinda Gates Foundation is among the most egregious of offenders—and have now persuaded others to do their dirty-work. In late 2011 young teachers in Los Angeles founded a chapter of the New York City-based Educators 4 Excellence (E4E). Members have signed a declaration calling for linking teacher evaluations to student test scores and for terminating policies that allow the least veteran teachers to be laid off first. The Bill & Melinda Gates Foundation, for example, awarded E4E about $1 million and Teach Plus—another such organization—about $4 million (Banchero 2011, December 1, A6).

21 Ninety years ago, even Franklin Bobbitt (1918, 3) allowed "the presence in the field of two antagonistic schools of educational thought. On the one hand are those who look primarily to the subjective results: the enriched mind, quickened appreciations, refined sensibilities, discipline, culture. To

DOI: 10.1057/9781137303424

them the end of education is the *ability to live* rather than the practical *ability to produce.*" Clearly the latter has triumphed. Even Bobbitt's conception of the practical—"those who hold that education is to look primarily and consciously to efficient practical action in a practical world"—was broader than it is today. Bobbitt (1918, 3) wrote: "The individual is educated who can perform efficiently the labors of his calling; who can effectively cooperate with his fellows in social and civic affairs; who can keep his bodily powers at a high level of efficiency; who is prepared to participate in a proper range of desirable leisure occupations; who can effectively bring his children to full-orbed manhood and womanhood; and who can carry on all his social relations with his fellows in an agreeable and effective manner. Education is consciously to prepare for these things." Ninety years ago, you note, "practicality" was not reduced to vocational preparation nor could the achievement of these aspirations—civic cooperation, health, thoughtful leisure, parenting, common courtesy—be assessed by standardized test scores. Can there be any doubt we are living now in an educational "dark age?"

22   Would that parents in the US express their outrage as did parents in Hong Kong, where tens of thousands assembled on the streets to protest the introduction of Chinese national education in Hong Kong schools. Critics liken the new curriculum to "brainwashing," observing that it "glosses over" major events like the Cultural Revolution and the Tiananmen Square massacre (Lau 2012, July 30, A4). It will be introduced in elementary schools in September 2012 and become mandatory for all public schools by 2016.

23   Such "electivism" was a consequence of a broader "progressivism" (whose history Ravitch rewrites) that, presumably, weakened the academic standards of US schools. At one point Ravitch (2000, 410) allows that there were many reasons for the decline in SAT scores—her main piece of empirical evidence for the "crisis" in US public schools—and among these were a "weakening of families and communities and the distracting effects of television, but there was also the stubborn fact that students were not taking as many academic courses as they had before the mid-1960s." So taking non-academic courses—what were they? how many were enrolled and of those how many then took the SAT?—is more influential than the "weakening of families and communities" (never mind television)? Evidence please!

24   The replacement of citizens with consumers is well-known in the destruction of democracy, but Karen Ferneding (2010, 178) suggests that the consumer is not an "actor" but a "chooser." Choosing among commodities requires no imagination (Ferneding 2010, 182)—or intellect I would add—primarily impulse. Its effect is the political passivity and ethical dissolution satiation invites. "The parallels between neo-liberalism and Huxley's *Brave New World* are remarkable," Grimmett and Young

DOI: 10.1057/9781137303424

(2012, 17 n. 6) point out: "In *Brave New World*, constant consumption is the bedrock of stability for the World State."

25   Scholarships were awarded to Hang Jing Qiu, Shirley LaVarco, Bianca Duah, Solomon Ajasin, Yvonne Cha, Farhana Nabi, Queen Adesuyi and Khalil Drayton (Berger 2012, February 25, A16).

DOI: 10.1057/9781137303424

2

Intellectual Histories

Abstract: *I summarize the ascendancy of the concept of "power" in US curriculum studies since 1968, arguing that the field's preoccupation with the concept reproduced the political defeat school reform represented. With the public school curriculum no longer under its jurisdiction, the field turned from "curriculum development" to "understanding curriculum," a reconceptualization of the function of the field that engendered new concepts, among them "reproduction theory" and, later, "resistance theory." Efforts to understand curriculum as primarily political were challenged in the 1980s by scholars arguing that race or gender were more primary that politics, but these new preoccupations with "identity" and, later (with the arrival of postmodernism in the late 1980s), "discourse" retained the previous preoccupation with power. Now widely accepted, these discourses are no longer intellectual provocations but background assumptions, and I argue they cannot convey the specificity of the circumstances surveyed in chapter 1. New concepts—including those from international and Jewish studies—can help structure the coming reconceptualization of the field.*

Pinar, F. William. *Curriculum Studies in the United States: Present Circumstances, Intellectual Histories.* New York: Palgrave Macmillan, 2013. DOI: 10.1057/9781137303424.

DOI: 10.1057/9781137303424

> To recall a product of intellectual breakthrough while forgetting the analytic conditions of its utterance is to have the answer but no memory of the question.
>
> Charles David Axelrod (1979, 1)

After the resounding defeat of 1968, it was no surprise that many of my generation positioned *power* as the crucial concept in understanding curriculum (see Pinar 2011a, 25–38). The conservative restoration has meant not only the dismantling of the New Deal but of public education as well. No wonder "power" appealed as an analytic concept! Recall that in the first paradigmatic moment—typified by Tyler's Rationale—political analyses had not predominated. Despite the superior scholarship of Dewey, Counts, Rugg, and Brameld, it was Tyler's Rationale that took center stage in curriculum studies. It would be proceduralism not analyses of power that would conceptually structure curriculum development. Severed from schools by the 1960s national curriculum reform, the field's reconceptualization soon focused on power. Neo-Marxism was openly embraced as informing analyses of power and critiques of ideology (Pinar et al. 1995, 243–246).

The vagueness of the concept of "power" contributed to its expansiveness. It inflated like a hot-air balloon, lifting its adherents far above the details of daily life, that last phrase a central category of curriculum research in Brazil (as noted: see Pinar 2011b, 206–209). From those heights, abstractions like "reproduction" and "resistance" summarized the sphere of the social, including the relationship between school and society. Political theorists came to realize that reproduction theory implied passivity, and so they coupled it with resistance, a concept implying agency (Pinar et al. 1995, 253). Within the panoramic concept of power, however, individual acts of agency[1] seemed tiny, even illusory. No longer individuals, US teachers were converted into "conduits" of neo-liberal ideology (Pinar 2011a, 33). Only the political theorists themselves exercised agency from their perch outside the world they claimed to describe. By failing to address the interpellation of the human subject, concepts such as "reproduction" became totalizing. They devalued individuals as epiphenomenal, in practical terms passive, relegated to resistance in a system they could not change but could only criticize. Through such dereferentialization, these concepts—reproduction and resistance—reenacted in the theoretical sphere the general outcomes of

DOI: 10.1057/9781137303424

1968 and the erasure of educational experience that the calamity called "school reform" ensured (see Pinar 2011a, 25–38).

At first subsumed within efforts to understand curriculum as political, the concept of race declared its sovereignty with the publication of Cameron McCarthy's 1990 *Race and Curriculum*. While focused on racial inequality, understanding curriculum as racial text was not as sovereign as it asserted, as it still privileged "power." "Race" substituted for a totalizing conception of power. For instance, Ladson-Billings and Tate (1995, 50) insisted that, while "untheorized," race[2] must be the primary category in efforts to understand "educational inequality." Never mind gender or class, never mind nation, never mind history. The Reardon research—referenced earlier in the survey of present circumstances—contradicts empirically the assertion that race is now the primary category for understanding inequality, however accurate the assertion of its primacy may have been 15 years ago. Identity politics, not empirical findings, were in play then, evident in Ladson-Billings and Tate's (1995, 61) rejection of any multiculturalism associated with "diversity" and its abstract celebration of "difference": indeed they reasserted the centrality of "race" by aligning their scholarship with Marcus Garvey (1996, 62), a figure synonymous with separatist racial politics and traditional gender hierarchies (Van Deburg 1997, 43). The reductionism of curriculum to its racial significance meant that theorists worked within their own particularism, asserting its primacy in understanding inequality or prejudice or oppression generally. Never mind specific situations or particular historical moments wherein race may not play the central role.

Nicole Guillory's (2010, 220) analysis of female black rappers demonstrates the "underlying intersections of, and sometimes tensions among race, class, generation, and sexuality." This sophisticated theoretical work shows as well how public pedagogy, in this central instance at least, demands that "teachers"—black female rappers in Guillory's research—decline to become uncritically culturally responsive, but in fact contest culture and demand its reconstruction. The black female rappers Guillory studied "talked back"—not only to white but also to black stereotypes of African-American women (2010, 220). Eschewing the cult of victimhood, Guillory's scholarship makes clear that reparation requires the subjective and social reconstruction of the colonized as well as the colonizing classes. Subjectivity and subject position are reciprocally related.[3]

DOI: 10.1057/9781137303424

Despite its distinctive history and terminology, efforts to understand curriculum as gendered text also incorporated "power" as central to many of its analyses. The essentialism of the early work became complicated by the early 1980s with racial critiques, but even among poststructuralists who arrived by the end of that decade the play of power remained central, even when it was inverted in those assertions that discourse could change social reality because reality too was fundamentally discursive. There were crucial exceptions to this tendency in the still resounding scholarship of Madeleine R. Grumet (1988), Janet L. Miller (2005), and Peter M. Taubman (1982). While women's studies may now be in eclipse—feminist theorist Patti Lather pronounced feminism a "dinosaur discourse" (2007, 12; see also 2007, 73)—a more sophisticated and historically nuanced concept of "woman" remains for many a key category (see Hendry 2011). While recent work emphasizes the cultural specificity of any identity named "woman," there remains an emphasis upon reparation and emancipation. Any obsessive concern over essentialism ensures its reproduction, if in anti-essentialist language. One startling illustration is Sara Carrigan Wooten's misreading of autobiographical remembrance for biological reductionism (see 2011, 321). "Inasmuch as we ritually decry essentialism," Henry Louis Gates Jr. (1990, 323) pointed out 20 years ago, "we remain conceptually sutured to it." Even the question of "queer," a conception that started as anti-identitarian (Jagose 1996, 83; Whitlock 2010, 269) now often privileges political correctness, group membership and the authority of experience.

As in efforts to understand curriculum as political text, then, over the past decades categories key to efforts to understand curriculum as gendered text—*identity* and *experience* most conspicuously—have also tended toward dereferentialization, devolving into abstractions detached from the demarcating details of the quotidian, from the temporality of history. In fact, each curriculum discourse—informed by political theory, racial theory, women's and gender studies—threatened to erase individual agency as each reified key concepts and emphasized a collective victimhood in the reproduction of power. Also severed from the specificity of lived experience, resistance—first asserted as an affirmation of agency—was soon relocated to a sphere of dereferentialized abstraction: quixotic, a gesture without consequence, embedded in a conceptual recycling of assertions of assault, injury, and victimization. In identity politics, power prevails, producing demoralizing generalizations if reiterated with positive valences: think of Sande Grande's (2004, 33)

DOI: 10.1057/9781137303424

neologism "whitestream thinkers" for example.[4] "This time," Rey Chow (2002, 112) points out, "we are confronted not with the forgetting of the racial origins of theory (and their multicultural implications) but rather with the reification of culture in the name of opposing 'theory' and opposing reification." Significantly, Chow (2002 113) adds: "in the name of precisely sponsoring the 'marginal,' the study of non-Western cultures would simply contribute toward a new, or renewed, Orientalism."

The reinstallation of discredited concepts in inverted forms is also evident in some instances of contemporary queer theory.[5] In his eagerness to absolve gay men of any allegations of self-destructiveness in their practice of high-risk sex (see 2009, 94)—allegations he worries reinscribe condemnations of gay sex as pathological—David Halperin ascribes to social "abjection" a "transformative power" (2009, 87), recasting it as not "the problem... but the solution" (2009, 87). Despite this effort to invert abjection's effects, Halperin (2009, 85, emphasis added) remains mired in the cynicism reproduction theory ensures:

> Agency does not emerge here as the natural outcome of a developmental process, the unfolding of a psychic structure, a constitutive property of the subject. It is rather than an *effect* of the play of social power: the unpredictable result of struggle.

No longer conceivable as a "cause," agency can now *only* be an "effect." As such, agency disappears, converted to "outcome." And as Nathalia Jaramillo (2010, 225) observes (in another context): "Discourse cannot disinter the body from where it is concretely located."

Forty years ago, the concept of "power" was a Marxist-inspired intervention into the apolitical proceduralism that structures the Tyler Rationale. Twenty years later the concept of "identity" contested an economistic Marxism that had claimed class as the only marker of inequality. No longer individual, identity splintered into cultural or gendered particularisms, as each minoritized group claimed reparation according to its own distinct history of violence, exclusion and trauma. Each effort advanced our understanding of curriculum as culturally variegated, historically informed, psychically saturated. Now, however, these concepts threaten to annul agency by collectivizing identity and totalizing power, erasing the singularity of students and teachers who can now only be construed as "conduits" of economic or racialized or gendered reproduction. As communism was for Joseph McCarthy's in the 1950s, power is everywhere, including the bedroom. Yet somehow

DOI: 10.1057/9781137303424

those who testify to the reproduction of power seem safely split off in some separate sphere of inoculated omniscience.

Efforts to understand curriculum as postmodern, poststructuralist, and deconstructed text also face the conceptual exhaustion that comes with their success. Once a historically informed intervention into the linearity, proceduralism and positivism of modernity (see Doll 1993), postmodernism—and its analytic children: poststructuralism and deconstruction—are now asserted as indisputable reality. Once again dereferentialization inflates concrete insights into new "grand narratives" (Lather 2007, 69). No longer a fact of life with which we grapple, uncertainty is now asserted as an ideal (see Pinar 2011a, 204, n. 2). Apparently we can never, however momentarily or situationally, be certain of anything (Lather 2007, 76), except, of course, of uncertainty. Is this not, as, Radhakrishnan (2008, 38) terms it, "fetishizing undecidability"? At one point Lather admonishes us to embrace "not-knowing" (2007, 7), as if ignorance were our new calling. Emphasizing the discursive character of historical narrative (see Roberts 1995, 255–256), some have insisted that history is fictional, an important (if partial) insight, but surely also an exaggeration that, if true, would render the history of misogyny (for instance) itself a fabrication. Other categories once central to education—among them rationality, progress, knowledge—are now discredited.[6] While no reasonable person would dispute the demand that these concepts require reconstruction, for some they are now only "targets" (Lather, 2007, 64). The destruction of "grand narratives" seems to have ensured only the resurrection of new "grand narratives," if now in different terminological forms.

Because these discourses have become widely accepted they are now ingrained in the mainstream assumptions of the US field. To assert them as somehow still "new" requires their endless radicalization,[7] stretching them from provocative insight into a specific situation into a nomological law that is everywhere and always true, even when that "law" decrees there are no laws. The concepts that once reconceptualized the US field—power, identity, discourse—appear to have played themselves out, signaled by tendencies toward totalization, reductionism and self-referentiality.[8] Like the positivism these concepts were intended to replace, once again researchers are somehow exempt from their embeddedness in the reality they purport to depict. There are practical as well as epistemological effects. If the subject is dispersed and power is primary, we are helpless to act. If uncertainty is our ideal, we wouldn't know what to

DOI: 10.1057/9781137303424

do even if the opportunity presented itself. If reproduction rules the day, there can be no justice: only cynicism and self-promotion are sensible. If my cultural or racial or gendered identity is paramount, the content of my character is irrelevant. It's every "man" for himself.

That last phrase seems somehow quintessentially American, even in its gendered inappropriateness. That rugged individualism—in the nineteenth century conveying the fantasy of the "self-made man" (Kimmel 1996, 67–69, 76)—may have morphed into metrosexual entrepreneurship, but it's still everyone for herself. Now competition and accumulation occur through collaboration, ever-increasing productivity, and above all technological innovation. While these interrelated organizational and economic developments are hardly restricted to any one country, they do seem far along in the US. In order to continue the effort to understand curriculum internationally, one must relinquish the business of imports and exports as well as the tourist's assumption that seeing is believing. Our concepts cannot comprehend what is outside them (Pinar 2011d, 1–2). Nor is what we find elsewhere capable of commodification for resale in America. The point of internationalization is not exploitation but self-excavation.

Such complicated conversation occurs within specific situations and historical moments. In the United States I sense that once again we are entering a phase of reconceptualization. I have offered (Pinar 2008) the concept of "internationalization" as a placeholder for what might occur during the "next moment" after this phase of "post-reconceptualization." The concept of "internationalization" structures the search but does not thematize the destination. By juxtaposing present circumstances and intellectual histories, I am underscoring that we must "work through" the present, not instrumentalize our way "forward." The future is elsewhere, in both historical and geographical terms. Supplementing the solidarity that the old Communist concept "internationalism" promised, internationalization singularizes our situation by requiring that self-understanding we aspire to communicate to others as we inhabit the "commons" is the field worldwide.

Notes

1   Cultural studies generally, Anderson and Valente (2002, 14) observe, seemed to have made "agency detection among the apparently disempowered the

DOI: 10.1057/9781137303424

overriding priority of its enterprise." What appears among the subaltern was denied to the visible, e.g. teachers.

2   The assertion of "race"—and its more encompassing conceptual cousin "culture"—as totalizing seems strange given Martin Luther King, Jr.'s famous 1963 demand that a person be judged by the content of his character, not by the color of his skin. Identity politics reinscribed racialist concepts while inverting their valence. One casualty is the concept of "character" (see Pinar 2011a, 10–11) left to be appropriated by cultural conservatives. Interracial collaboration is also a casualty, contradicting the history of civil rights struggle generally and the intellectual formation of key African-American intellectuals specifically (see Posnock 1998).

3   For the descendants of colonizers, some form of self-shattering (Pinar 2006b) must characterize at least the initial stages of subjective reconstruction. For descendents of the colonized, some affirmation of indigenous culture is obviously appropriate, but as a moment in working through the effects of colonization. Recall that Sartre endorsed *négritude* as just such a moment, a judgment with which Fanon at first struggled, then accepted (Hansen 1977, 34; Mercer 1994, 298). To decolonize the curriculum starts but cannot end in either self-shattering or self-affirmation, as working through the past engenders provides passage to a future we cannot foresee.

4   My critique of identity politics is specific, namely its tendency to collectivize identity and alienate political allies, what I have termed "strategically dysfunctional essentialism" (2009). Clearly, political interventions linked to identity remain essential in specific locales on specific occasions. The curriculum censorship legislated in Arizona is a case in point. On January 1, 2012, after a new state law focused on Mexican-American studies courses that had been criticized as anti-white was upheld. Michael Winerip (2012, March 19, A8) reports that it became illegal to teach *Mexican WhiteBoy* by Matt de la Peña in Tucson public school classrooms. State officials alleged that the book contained "critical race theory," a violation under a provision that prohibits lessons "promoting racial resentment." Paulo Freire's *Pedagogy of the Oppressed* was also banned. Not only books were censored, class lessons were as well, among them one entitled "From Cortes to Bush: 500 Years of Internalized Oppression" (quoted passages in 2012, March 19, A8). While that title seems overly expansive and threatens totalization, Arizona lawmakers' reaction affirms its timeliness.

5   Speaking of gay studies, Chauncey (2000, 305) blames not processes of "maturation" and "deferentialization" but institutionalization: "We also face the problem that any such institutionalization of intellectual inquiry threatens: namely, to reify and naturalize the very categories it was initially designed to critique, and to freeze a rapidly developing field at a particular moment in its evolution." That seems a fair statement of what has happened

DOI: 10.1057/9781137303424

with efforts to understand curriculum as political, racial, and gender text. It is important to remember, however, that institutionalization can enable as well as disarm intellectual critique.

6 John Willinsky is not afraid to affirm the ongoing significance of the (unfinished) Enlightenment. "Enlightenment," he (2006, 149) summarizes, "is about moving people out from under the tutelage of others. Enlightenment is furthered by a good education system, by all means, but it can only be sustained and made vital, I would dare to conclude from Kant's and Derrida's positions, by finding ways of increasing people's access to intellectual resources that would support the public reasoning and freedom Kant speaks of." Willinsky is not alone in associating the aspirations of the Enlightenment with open access. "[A] great part of the excitement of life in the post-Enlightenment period," Marilynne Robinson (2010, 3) points out, "has come with the thought that reality could be reconceived, that knowledge would emancipate humankind if only it could be made accessible to them. Such great issues, human origins and human nature, have the public as an appropriate theater, since the change they propose is cultural." And it should go without saying that the "public theater" includes the public school curriculum. It must not disappear online, but remain an assembly in which subjective presence renders academic study immediate and often improvisational.

7 Lather's "not-knowing" becomes for Springgay and Freeman (2010, 229) the "unthought" and a process of becoming that is "always incomplete," the latter term reiterating one thesis of the 1962 Association for Supervision and Curriculum Development yearbook. Not only history but subjectivity disappears in this embrace of "intercorporeal understandings" and "an intimate curriculum" (Springgay and Freeman 2010, 231). While "touching" (2010, 231) is an intriguing concept, its ethicality is not obvious despite the authors' assertion (2010, 237). That is one of Murray's (2010, 240) points (elaborated in his response), namely that touching and being-touched are ambiguous in their meaning; the body requires thinking and articulation (2010, 242; see Gershon 2011). Despite its promise, in this essay radicalization overreaches itself.

8 Concepts appear (and/or reappear) as the conclusions of evidence, empirical or argumentative. (They can also reveal evidence, functioning as binoculars rendering visible other concepts have kept hidden. But in these instances too, the precision of referentialization is key.) When such evidence derives from lived experience and the historical moment (themselves intersecting concepts), there is that (possibly lasting) moment of resonance, as readers now have words for what before was experienced but not expressed, or perhaps not noticed at all. In adherence to the established concept, evidence becomes its extension, and the concept survives severed from its conception,

DOI: 10.1057/9781137303424

institutionalized through repetition, no longer provocative, only iconic. Like other slogans—LaCapra (2004, 211) is here discussing the educational embrace of "excellence"—"such concepts become formalistic floating signifiers—word-balloons without words—to be filled with any possible content, however gaseous." Deferentialization denotes, then, the severance of a concept from the specificity of its genesis; it loses its self-reconstructing link to the historical moment and devolves into self-referentiality, no longer provocative but an incantation, not a call to arms. In a Benjaminian sense, intellectual breakthrough represents "redeeming aspects of a past or present situation that may be reactivated, transvalued, or refunctioned and inserted into a significant different context" (LaCapra 2004, 211). That "redemption" is the reconstruction that constitutes intellectual advancement.

DOI: 10.1057/9781137303424

3

Reconceptualization

Abstract: *I specify—referencing the 2010* Curriculum
Studies Handbook: The Next Moment—*the conceptual
shifts that suggest that a second reconceptualization is
now underway. Through the hybridization of concepts
common in the reconceptualized field (1970–2000), a new
generation of scholars is consolidating the conceptual gains
made during those decades and now complicating them
as they attune them to present circumstances. "Woman"
remains as a concept, for instance, but now reformulated
as "nonunitary, situated, and always in flux." Technology
intensifies, and concepts such as "the posthuman" emerge
at the same time that historical and international studies
are achieving greater importance, as the field's past
and its presence within nationally specific and globally
situations demand increasing attention. I argue that the
internationalization and coming reconceptualization of
curriculum studies in the United States are reciprocally
related.*

Pinar, F. William. *Curriculum Studies in the United States:
Present Circumstances, Intellectual Histories.* New York:
Palgrave Macmillan, 2013. DOI: 10.1057/9781137303424.

> Our responsibility as curriculum theorists is to "bring out" the
> dead—to "respond" and engage in conversation with the past.
>
> Petra Munro Hendry (2011, 209)

Faced with excruciating external circumstances and having inherited
a series of totalizing assumptions severed from the singularities of the
present historical moment, the US field is living through a "next moment"
that is indeed difficult. Progress—what one day will be, I suspect, ret-
rospectively characterized as a second reconceptualization[1]—is, will be,
slow. While there is considerable, often intriguing, scholarly activity, the
internal structural problems that Kliebard (2000 [1970]a) identified four
decades ago—those ahistorical and ameliorative tendencies—have not
disappeared. There is more and often innovative historical research (as
I will reference momentarily), and that is heartening. But to formulate
new concepts, conceptual research is necessary, e.g. theoretical research
that is also historical (and vice versa), and such work remains in short
supply. Instead we suffer too many ethnographies, too many of which tell
us what we already know (for examples see Pinar 2011a, 147–149). There
is too much political correctness. Determined to decry "essentialism" or
"master narratives" or culturally unresponsive pedagogy condemns us to
pontification, not provocation. Our preoccupation with power has positioned us outside everyday life, incapable of enunciation, split-off from
the singularity of the situation. Dereferentialization invites incantation,
not intellectual breakthrough.

Within present circumstances—1) debilitating hostility externally,
including the destruction of the field's historic object of scholarship:
the public school, 2) conceptual exhaustion as the key concepts (power,
discourse, identity) fade from the foreground into background assumptions, and 3) internationalization—a third paradigmatic moment strug-
gles to start in the US. It is underway, however, and there are clues in
the 2010 *Curriculum Studies Handbook*. That landmark volume suggests
that the new paradigm, at least in its initial phases, may represent no
sharp shift from the second (as was the second to the first). In fact, this
shift to the third moment may prove to be somewhat continuous with
the second moment, perhaps even consolidating its theoretical gains. I
am suggesting that the function of the field may remain "understanding curriculum" even while its efforts to do so look rather different—
decidedly dialogic, often hybrid, even, like the Mexican curriculum field,
"polysemic" (see Pinar 2011d, 40)—from those described in *Understanding*

DOI: 10.1057/9781137303424

Curriculum (1995). As Madeleine Grumet (2010, 409) has noted, rather than "post-reconceptualization" the phrase "to be continued" may be more appropriate, as she is struck by the continuation, not the termination, of efforts to understand curriculum. The questions Nina Asher asks, Grumet (2010, 404) points out, are those "we asked 30 years ago, yet we hear them and answer them differently today."

Grumet's observation occurs at the end of her commentary on Nina Asher's 2010 *Handbook* chapter on decolonization, an example of a somewhat new concept—one incorporating class and culture while focused on the moment *after* political calamity—that functions to reconceptualize previous efforts to understand curriculum as political, racial, and internationalized. While the key concepts of the reconceptualization are now the background of what is being thought today, they have not disappeared. They are discernible in Asher's (2010, 397) question: "How, then, do we decolonize curriculum so that it enables us to deconstruct such binaries as self and other, margins and center so that the self unlearns the internalization of the oppressor?" Note the juxtaposition of terms associated with each concept: "deconstruct" and "binaries" reiterate the poststructuralist emphasis upon discourse, and there is a reincorporation of the autobiographical concepts of "self" and "other" but this time linked with postcolonial ideas of "margin" and "center" that recast historically political analyses of power (e.g. as "oppression"). What prompts Grumet to recover the genesis of her work with me on teacher education and autobiography (see Grumet 2010, 403) is, I suspect, Asher's positioning of "unlearning" as central to curriculum. It was acknowledgment of this problem of unlearning—one that is affective as well as cognitive, embodied as well as political—that led us to emphasize the reconstruction (what Grumet casts as "aesthetic" forms) of subjectivity.[2] The internal dynamics of unlearning are indicated in Asher's (2010, 398) citation of Ross Mooney: "Death sensed/Is source again."

Even in claims of the "new," one hears echoes of the old. While the data reported in first section isolated economic factors in school reform, Adam Howard and Mark Tappan argue, importantly, that these must be understood as also social and psychic. Acknowledging that class and schooling have often been associated, Howard and Tappan (2010, 326) suggest that to advance toward a "new theoretical terrain" we must forefront "social, cultural, and personal" rather than "economic" factors in understanding how social class "shapes" educational experience. Given Howard's life history—at least as he reports it in the introduction to

DOI: 10.1057/9781137303424

his *Learning Privilege: Lessons of Power and Identity in Affluent Schooling* (Howard 2008)—one would think he and Tappan would emphasize not only how social class *shapes* educational experience, but also how social class can be *reconstructed by* educational experience. Instead of affirming agency, Howard and Tappan (2010, 327) risk reinscribing the determinism of reproduction theory by asserting that social class is "defined" by "social conditions." It seems that *everything*—Howard and Tappan list (2010, 327) "knowing" and "doing," as well as "values, beliefs, assumptions," as well as "relations with others" and the "world around them"—"reflect[s]" their social class. At this point "new theoretical terrain" sounds rather like the old one. Only at the end of their chapter do Howard and Tappan (2010, 329) "note" that we are not "simply automatons, blindly following cultural and ideological dictates and scripts." If not "simply automatons," what might we be? Sensing the reductionism, Ellen Brantlinger (2010, 337) writes in her response to their chapter: "Because I fault Howard and Tappan for not sufficiently refining their concept of identity to exclude its use by deficit theorists, I make use of Freire's term emancipation to delimit the construct." It is clear that for Brantlinger (see 2010, 338), emancipation implies "agency," the construct gone missing in the Howard-Tappan analysis.

That the new paradigmatic moment may represent in its first phase both consolidation of its antecedent moments and an effort to exceed them is also evident in the recent research of Petra Munro Hendry, wherein what was before distinct discourses—efforts to understand curriculum as historical, as gendered, as poststructuralist—becomes, as our Brazilian and Mexican colleagues might say, hybridized, reassembled in something we have not seen before. "To focus solely on gender analysis suffers like all other theoretical constructs in that it is a closed system," Hendry (2011, 206) concludes at the end of her *Engendering Curriculum History*. "Woman" remains as a concept, if now as "nonunitary, situated, and always in flux" (Hendry 2010, 496).[3] For me, identity politics erases history in its reification of culture and in the presentism of its political preoccupations (see Pinar 2009, 22). But for Hendry (2010, 499) "identity politics is deeply embedded in historical consciousness." If the "flux" that Hendry identifies is historical and not a presentistic reshuffling of opportunities occasioned by injury, then Hendry is indeed providing passage to a next moment wherein the specificity of subjectivity and situation can be threaded through politics. Certainly such passage is evident in her recovery of Jane Addams' engagement with questions of

DOI: 10.1057/9781137303424

race (Munro 1999, 42). Through that groundbreaking research, Hendry anticipated the current fascination with "public pedagogy" (Sandlin, Schultz and Burdick 2010). "In extending educational sites to settlement houses and women's clubs," Munro [Hendry] (1999, 43) concludes, "these women sought to promote a vision of education that was community-based, lifelong, and directed toward social equality." What now risks devolving into a slogan—"social justice"[4]—is rendered here in histori-cally specific and gendered terms that affirms that the past is where we might find the future.

As the stunning scholarship of Bernadette Baker (2001) suggests, studying the past discloses the present, particularly its focus on the pub-lic school and "childhood-as-rescue" (2010, 345). The former can be a decoy concept, substituting an institution for the process it presumably houses, while the latter restates a Christian condemnation of infancy as wicked and requiring redemption. The emphasis on "school" has meant an endless tinkering with organizational matters—scheduling, test-ing, assessment—and an apparently unconscious incapacity to attend to the educational experience of these forms. There is a conflation of "molds" and "spirit" (Pinar 2011a, 77). Baker's undertaking—informed by poststructuralism and postcolonialism as well as history—is more ambitious, showing how "animal magnetism, mesmerism, and hypnosis infused the production of scientific objects, including belief in mind as a legitimate site of engineering; [and] the classification of children" (Baker 2010, 344).

Baker reminds us that William James devoted 20 years to the study of "psychic phenomena" such as mediumship, telepathy, and automatic writing (2010, 351–352). What this research reveals, Baker (2010, 362) explains, is that curriculum history itself cannot be confined to the history of a "particular institution," and that a "new series of questions" present themselves that require reconsideration of our historic devotion to the public school and to childhood-as-rescue, as these two categories may have less to do with engineering social democracy and more to do with convoluted residues of nineteenth-century preoccupations with redemption, asserted through therapy and imperialism (2010, 362; see also Baker 2009, 38).

As does Bernadette Baker's (2002), Annie Winfield's research empha-sizes how the past structures the present, in this instance how eugenics remains, if unrecognized, today. Winfield's research is at once curricu-lum history, political critique, and racial analysis. Emphasizing Franklin

DOI: 10.1057/9781137303424

Bobbitt's early and—Winfield (2010, 151) argues—continuing acceptance of eugenics, Winfield (2010, 153) demands: "How far have we come? To what extent does ideological residue coat our own imaginings and filter the light that might be?" She identifies an "ideological throughline" (2010, 154) that shows that the "sorting, testing, and tracking developed by eugenicists is rooted in the melding of scientific efficiency with educational objectives" (2010, 152). The racist genesis of US curriculum studies, Winfield insists, persists, most prominently in Tyler's rationale, forefronting objectives as a "basic principle" of curriculum development, and linking "objectives" with "assessment." The prominence of race in the 1970s Reconceptualization of the field may, then, have not only been a complex consequence of changes in society (e.g. the civil rights movement), but an internally prompted ethical demand to divest the field of those traces of eugenics that remained.

Efforts to understand curriculum racially have intensified and proliferated in focus and function. There remains, however, as Denise Taliaferro-Baszile (2010, 484) asserts, the "lack of Black voices" in curriculum studies. Few, I think, would disagree that Carter Woodson[5] is among those Black voices who has been marginalized in the mainstream field. Few would disagree that he is a more apt icon of the "racial subject" (Taliaferro-Baszile 2010, 484) than Marcus Garvey, as LaVada Brandon's scholarship makes plain. Remembered as a "reconceptualist, a historian, and a profound education philosopher" (Brandon 2010, 126), Woodson sought through the study of African-American history a "*real education* [that] would elicit a new consciousness to arise in African American people" (2010, 125). Facts engender consciousness, an educational process of decolonization (see Brandon 2010, 130) requiring subjective reconstruction. "Woodson held," Brandon (2010, 131) explains, "that self-determination and democratization of one's own psyche were critical components of real education." Contemporary scholars such as Cornel West, Angela Davis, Patricia Hill Collins, Darlene Clark Hine, and Vanessa Siddle Walker, Theodora Berry (2010, 141) points out, "can all trace their roots as organic intellectuals to this particular period of African American scholarship." Acknowledging the founding roles that Woodson, Du Bois, Washington played, Berry (2010, 140) emphasizes the centrality of Mary Church Terrell, Mary McLeod Bethune, Anna Julia Cooper, and Pauli Murray as key "contributors of African American educational thought." The aforementioned scholarship of Nichole Guillory, like that of Brandon and

DOI: 10.1057/9781137303424

Taliaferro-Baszile, sheds the incapacitating passivity reproduction theory had installed.[6]

Missing still in the US field is adequate acknowledgment of indigenous knowledge and wisdom as well as commemorations of the genocide—the effects of which still resound today, acknowledgment that is central in curriculum studies in Canada (Ng-A-Fook and Rottmann 2012; Stanley and Young 2011; Hampton 1995). Sande Grande's (2004) engagement with critical pedagogy may raise more questions than it answers, but *Red Pedagogy* is an important provocation that US scholars are obligated to address. And the important work conducted by Asian-American and Latino/a, Chicano/a, and other minoritized scholars remains split-off from curriculum studies' conception of itself (see Rodriguez and Kitchen 2004).

Efforts to recuperate other traditions of disavowed knowledge are underway, as the recent reclamation of psychoanalysis by Peter Taubman (2011) accomplishes. The work of Deborah Britzman, Alice Pitt, and Jennifer Gilbert has never been marginal in my own thinking, but Taubman shows how the scientism of US academic psychology and the authoritarianism of US "school reform" displaced psychoanalysis from the very public stage it once held. The recurring question of the human subject—culturally variable, politically interpellated, historically situated, and regionally placed—is being inventively reformulated in the United States by Hongyu Wang (2004), Ugena Whitlock (2007, 2010), and Brian Casemore (2008).

When Madeleine Grumet and I first encouraged teachers to speak of their lived experience in classrooms (see Pinar and Grumet 2006 [1976]), the first-person singular was still banned in standard composition practices and self-reference was considered questionable in classroom discourse. Four decades ago it took courage and encouragement for students—preservice and practicing teachers—to talk about themselves. Now it seems many can talk about little else. "[I]f we ourselves are the *sole* question," Stuart Murray (2010, 242–243) reminds, "there can be no other orientating question, no other, no Archimedean point from to pose the question that 'we ourselves' somehow *are*." What rescues autobiography in education—surely Grumet (2010, 404) is right, after decades of identity politics and the world-at-risk, to "welcome back the individual to curriculum"—is its capacity for referentialization. The immediacy of lived experience—rarely transparent, always in the shadow of the other—embodies thinking as it specifies situations and affirms

DOI: 10.1057/9781137303424

relationality. Except when confined in a narcissistic embrace—always a danger, evidenced in the compulsion to make everything self-referenced (see Slattery 2010)—autobiography reaches outward toward the world. "[I]n curriculum," Grumet (2010, 407) reminds, "we point to the world worth knowing."

The canonical curriculum question—*what knowledge is of most worth?*—is also an autobiographical question. It is a racial question as well. "Critical race *currere*," as Denise Taliaferro-Baszile (2010, 492) conceives the phrase, seeks to "signify...the racialized extended-self and the meanings it makes of education for liberation." In African-American autobiography—from slave narratives to the present-day—the subjective and the social are interrelated (Pinar 2004, 40–46). And in Critical Race Theory, Taliaferro-Baszile (2010, 492) points out, the Black autobiographic voice is construed as a "counter-storyteller." Efforts to understand curriculum racially, politically, and autobiographically become reconstructed in critical race *currere* which, Taliaferro-Baszile (2010, 492 explains, "emphasizes the significance of race—and to some extent as it intersects with class, gender, sexuality and other subjectivities—in shaping oneself and one's educational experiences." Here is the dynamic—the "mutually constituting"—interplay between subjectivity and subject position (Grumet 2010, 407).

Although Taliaferro-Baszile does not use the phrase, perhaps "double-consciousness" is one consequence of racialization. W. E. B. Du Bois was referencing the complicated subject position of African-Americans, but given contemporary restatements of "correctional education" (Pinar 2012, 99–101) such as *Race to the Top*, perhaps every educator, whatever her identity, might cultivate the capacity to see both through one's eyes *and* through the eyes of others. Such a double-consciousness structures the quiet refusal to comply with *Race to the Top*. Perhaps because the arts hold such strong potential for "interrupting history," as Tom Barone (2010, 480) points out, they have been excluded by the Obama administration's obsessive association of education with the economy and its curricular privileging of science, technology, engineering, and mathematics.[7]

Douglas McKnight (2010, 501, 509, 511) addresses the "despair" that federal and state educational policies leave in their wake; he does so by reconstructing *currere* as "passionate inwardness"[8] in which "ethics" is central. Such working from within (Pinar 1972) provides, McKnight (2010, 502) understands, a "reflexive means...to exist within and even move beyond such enclosures [e.g. restrictive policies]." He concludes:

DOI: 10.1057/9781137303424

"To situate oneself in this way opens more spaces within the institution that point toward a 'smaller,' more attentive, more subtle existence within the classroom." The concept of "resistance" cannot convey the subtly and situatedness of such activism.[9]

Endorsing posthumanism[10], Nathan Snaza (2010, 50) links that concept with "ethics" and the capacity to "think something other than identity." He suggests Deleuze's concept of "singularity," which for him means "thinking love and ethics together"[11] toward the formation of "community."[12] While singularity evokes the autobiographical, for Deleuze the concept is more panoramic, as it seems to reference reality itself. The world, Deleuze (1993, 60) asserts, "*is a pure emission of singularities*." For Deleuze (1993, 63), "that is the real definition of the individual: concentration, coincidence of a certain number of converging pre-individual singularities." Subjectivity here is simultaneously focused and infinite, its coherence a questionable (rather than necessary) illusion. Indeed: "There is no primacy of the individual; there is instead an indissolubility of a singular Abstract and a collective Concrete" (Deleuze and Guattari 1987, 100).

For Snaza (2010, 52), to be "posthuman...is to learn to live aesthetically," but posthuman aesthetics is not what Maxine Greene (2001) deems central to educational experience. "Posthumanism emerges," Hal Foster (2005, 10) explains, "when technology does in fact 'become me,' not by being incorporated into my organic unity and integrity, but instead by interrupting that unity and opening the boundary between self and world." That threatens subjective dissolution, an entirely dystopian definition of "posthumanism," as Foster's (2005, 69) analysis of cyberpunk fiction asserts: "there is nothing inherently progressive in the denaturalization of the idea of 'the body.'" Indeed, Foster (2005, 74) concludes that "cyberpunk insists on the subjection of all individuals to preexisting systems of control and power." Technoculture can be totalizing.

Critical studies of "the posthuman acceptance of the technological mediation of embodiment and subjectivity" (Foster 2005, 72) may become central in the field to come. Here the Canadian critiques and celebrations of technoculture are central to understanding technoculture anywhere. The groundbreaking work of Harold Innis, George Grant, Marshall McLuhan and Margaret Atwood are indispensable in understanding the dystopian present. In her chilling chapter in the 2010 *Handbook*, Karen Ferneding (2010, 172) construes technology as arising from "humanity's quest for transcendence and salvation." Ferneding references David Noble, but George Grant would do as well, and within

DOI: 10.1057/9781137303424

curriculum studies, the canonical work of James B. Macdonald (1995) addresses this point.[13]

Ferneding (2010, 173) situates technology historically, citing the railroad as the "predecessor" of information and computer technologies (ICT), as also "infrastructure" that renders "space superfluous," arguments also made by Innis and McLuhan.[14] Space[15] is nowhere and everywhere, and virtuality replaces experience (2010, 174). In the technological acceleration of time,[16] the future is already past, as Ferneding's (2010, 175) reference to Ernest Jünger (and Pinar 2012, 168–170) implies. Like Snaza, Ferneding (2010, 175) acknowledges the arrival of the posthuman, but (like me) she does not welcome it, characterizing it, after Baudrillard, as the "perfect crime," in which technoculture discards the human *and* any evidence of having done so. "The technological system," Ferneding (2010, 176) concludes, "becomes a tautology that initiates the end of mystery." Returning to her initial association of technology and transcendence, Ferneding (2010, 180) wonders what can be the "meaning of transcendence within postmodern technoculture?" Does it devolve into "perpetual virtual self-reconstruction" (2010, 182)? Does the body disappear into an avatar?

There are other discourses influential now, sustainability perhaps primary among them (see Riley-Taylor 2010, Hensley 2011, Bowers 1995, 2000, 2001, 2005). Arts-based research is hardly peripheral.[17] But this monograph can be no comprehensive survey. Here I am focused on the indicators of reconceptualization in signs of consolidation that at the same time surpass the present through reactivating the past. One sign is the synoptic text composed by João M. Paraskeva. Hybridity is the order of the day. Pertinent to the present discussion is that even Paraskeva's determination to contain in one "critical river" multiple currents of understanding curriculum politically floods its banks; he endorses an "itinerant curriculum theory" that asserts a "deliberate disrespect of the canon" (2011, 184). In Paraskeva's proclamation, this "river" has "gone south" (2011, 186). That South is Latin America, where we can avoid "any kind of Eurocentrism" (2011, 186) while not "romanticizing indigenous knowledge" (2011, 187). Into this "third space" the key concepts of "progressive curriculum scholars"—"hegemony, ideology, power, social emancipation, class, race, and gender"—must go so that we might "(re) address the towering questions of curriculum," starting (and ending, it turns out: see the final page of the text) with the one asked by Counts in 1932: "Dare the school build a new social order?" "Addressing this

DOI: 10.1057/9781137303424

question," Paraskeva (2011, 187) is sure, "implies a new thinking, a new theory...an itinerant curriculum theory." Traveling takes us back to familiar ground—Counts' question—and in so doing, the old becomes "new."

Itinerancy and constancy, old and new: what we want, it seems, is what George Tomkins, referencing the Canadian curriculum, character-ized as "stability" and "change." Such mutually interdependent dynamics of disequilibrium and reequilibration are nowhere more vividly enacted than in the "fascinating imaginative realm" of William E. Doll, Jr. (Trueit 2012). Referencing Richard Rorty, David L. Hall (1994, 50) suggested that "the postmodernist is the poignant figure of a rationalist in irrational times." Doll exemplifies such a figure. He began in Dewey and pragma-tism, which led him to Jean Piaget. But Doll was not leaving one for the other. Indeed, he integrated aspects of each thinker into his postmodern view of curriculum (see Doll 1993). Postmodernism made sense juxta-posed to modernity, that privileging of reason, and specifically science, over religion, coupled with the advent of capitalism, and its adversaries socialism and communism. In Doll's lexicon it specifies confidence in linear cause-and-effect rationality. For the sake of control and efficiency, as Doll's (1998, 2004, 2005) historical analyses makes clear, US schools curtail creativity. Creativity is one appeal of complexity theory for Doll, as it privileges the dynamism of curriculum and instruction. Doll's concepts—among them richness, recursivity, rigor and relationality, sup-plemented by his five Cs (*currere*, complexity, cosmology, conversation, and community)—summarize much of the conceptual work undertaken in the field over the past 40 years. Complexity theory (Doll et al. 2005) may even compete for center stage in the "next moment," including in Canada, at least if the widely-known work of William E. Doll, Jr. and that of Brent Davis, Dennis Sumara, and Rebecca Luce-Kapler (2000; Davis 2004) takes hold.

The labor of reconceptualization is the labor of rereferentialization, a process in which concepts from other disciplines, countries, cultural traditions, and historical moments enable us to enunciate the present moment, itself simultaneously unprecedented and utterly familiar. I have offered allegory (Pinar 2012, 49–52) to underscore the utterly unique and decidedly common character of our circumstances. There is allegorical element discernible in the pedagogy of our Idaho colleague Ann Rosenbaum, as she insists on ancient traditions of orality, also cel-ebrated in indigenous cultures (Pinar 2011a, 210 n. 23) and among many

DOI: 10.1057/9781137303424

Canadians (see Saul 2008) who, like Harold Innis,[18] have labored to learn from indigenous knowledge. Rosenbaum teaches (you recall) through questioning, a form of dialogical encounter that requires close reading, subjective coherence, self-expressivity, complicated conversation.

Obviously power *is* being reproduced by the aggressive incursion into the education of children by computer companies like Apple and Microsoft, but their effects are not only ideological. We do not yet know what life-on-screens means, but the initial research is not always encouraging (Pinar 2012, 143–152). And while we can also say that Idaho teachers' marches and the organization of the referendum represent "resistance," this term is too crude to convey a more specific dynamic at work, the assertion of vocation over politics. In my terms, these teachers are enacting a professional ethics of "intransigence" (Pinar 2012, 237–238) as they affirm the centrality of academic freedom—intellectual independence—in public education. Quite rightly they insist that if they are to practice their profession, the use of technology in their classrooms must remain a matter of their own professional discretion (Richtel 2012, January 4, B4). Since the reconceptualization it has been clear that the gender of the teaching profession is relevant in any analysis of power, as elected officials (who, in the *New York Times* report, are only male) feel quite entitled to intervene in teachers' professional practices with an aggressivity they dare not demonstrate with lawyers or physicians, professions gendered male in the public imagination. But is Ann Rosenbaum's *identity* as a woman central to understanding her decision to defy the Governor and the Legislature of the State of Idaho?

What is clear, given her remarks, is that Rosenbaum's action had everything to do with her conception of teaching. Indeed, this teacher's professional commitment to the centrality of "thinking" in teaching cannot be reduced to an instance of "resistance" or an effect of "discourse" or "identity." This educator's commitment to teaching students "to think deeply" enacts agency, a concept obscured in preoccupations with power and resistance, and rendered epiphenomenal when class and culture are cast as determinative. It is agency simultaneously individual and shared with students and colleagues. And its most significant expression may not be the march or even the referendum—important pronouncements of professional ethics even if they fail—but the everyday pedagogical engagement with students, enunciation within the sphere of the quotidian. Students' endorsement of their teachers' actions suggests their respect for the profession and that implies respect for their own academic

DOI: 10.1057/9781137303424

labor. Moreover, some students may now appreciate (perhaps not for first time) that thinking through study, not pressing keys on machines, comprises education.

As this episode indicates, the concepts which decades ago represented intellectual advancement—power, identity, discourse—remain salient. Most scholars working today accept their relevance; indeed, they assume them as true. Because they are now assumptions, these categories tell us nothing we didn't know already, and worse, they have come at quite a cost. Agency is one key conceptual casualty. The historical moment demands that we reclaim it, if now reconceptualized in terms that acknowledge the material realities of power, the haunting influence of identity, and determinations of discourse in agency's enactment.[19] Such enactment is simultaneously social and subjective, embedded in what Rubén Gaztambide-Fernández (2010, 79, 85) construes as "creative solidarity"—what Janet L. Miller (2010, 96) calls "communities without consensus"[20]—and expressive of one's subjective commitment to students, to colleagues, to the profession, in Peter Appelbaum's (2010, 462) phrase, "a greater sense of a larger common project in the post-reconceptual age."

Perhaps agency will not survive as a concept as its asocial psychologistic antecedents may prove too discrediting. A new concept—perhaps a hybrid term derived from Elizabeth Macedo's (2011) emphasis upon enunciation and resignification recalling Dewey's century-old concept of "reconstruction"—will be formulated that enables us to specify the singularity of the present moment. The coming reconceptualization of curriculum studies in the United States will occur, then, through reactivating past concepts attuned to present circumstances through the study of curriculum studies worldwide. Such study is not undertaken in the service of being able to present something "new" at the next conference, to "brand" oneself as "critical" or "radical" or "culturally responsive" (Moon 2011). We are called to concepts through changing circumstances. Those circumstances are local, as reports from Idaho underscore. Studying the intellectual histories and present circumstances of curriculum studies elsewhere—historically as well as geographically—enables us to appreciate just how "exceptional" the US situation is. With current concepts collapsing due to their widespread and uncritical acceptance, new concepts are required amidst the disciplinary demoralization of "post-reconceptualization." We cannot find the future in the present. It is not here but elsewhere: in the past, in Brazil, Mexico, South Africa.

DOI: 10.1057/9781137303424

It is in Canada. Each field has its own distinctive intellectual history, its own particular set of present circumstances, internal and external, often intersecting spheres (although that depends too on where and when). Through the formulation of temporally attuned and place-specific concepts we can compose concepts to convey what we now experience but cannot yet adequately articulate. The internationalization and reconceptualization of curriculum studies in the United States are reciprocally related. It is the former that will enable the latter.

Notes

1   "Fifteen years ago it might have been appropriate to identify discourses by way of gender" [etc.], Erik Malewski (2010, xiv) points out, underscoring the shift I am suggesting is now just underway. He continues: "Since then much has changed. Cultural studies, critical race theory, and critical geography have entered the field. Discourses that might in the past have been distinguishable have made their way into hybrid spaces that make their unique characteristics undeterminable. Queer theory, place, autobiography, and Southern studies combined to make the work of Ugena Whitlock, for example"(2010, xiv). Hybridity—a key concept in curriculum studies in Brazil—is a key marker, as Malewski suggests here.

2   Grumet (2010, 403) wonders whether she and I may have been "naïve" in our emphasis on an "aesthetic" sense of subjectivity, evident in our regular referencing of Virginia Woolf and Jerzy Grotowski. In my view, it is the aesthetic enactment of agency (through creativity) that remains crucial in reconstructing the present moment. Such reconstruction relies on collective, even ritualized, forms of action that have to be threaded through individual subjectivity. Thirty-five years ago that emphasis upon particularity kept Grumet and me from preoccupation with the reproduction of power. It protected us from identity politics, although later, as Grumet (2010, 403) notes, we both concentrated on subjectivity's debts to gender, race, and class. Curriculum theory, as Grumet (2010, 404) understood from the outset, contains questions that "lift the ideological drapes that hide these categories from consciousness." In this sense our "naïve" curriculum theory of many years ago installed decolonization as central in the project of self-understanding (Pinar 2011a, 39–48), even if we didn't use the term. In the structural non-coincidence between subjectivity and subject position, then, is opportunity for creativity, originality, agency.

3   On occasion this "nonunitary" sense of identity threatens subjective dissolution and with it the disappearance of agency. Significantly, Hongyu

DOI: 10.1057/9781137303424

Wang (2010, 379) points out: "While the center of the person is displaced, it is in this decentering that the possibility of personal freedom is situated."

4   Uncritical and ahistorical acceptance of the call for "social justice" reinscribes the same instrumental relation between school and society that school reformers invoke to scapegoat teachers and sell schools to software companies. The "claim that the achievement gap constitutes the gravest threat facing the US today appears hyperbolic if not absurd," Taubman (2009, 30) makes plain, "until, that is, we consider the number of educators who argue that if we had better teachers in schools and did a better job of educating our students, crime would go down, the economy would improve, and class divisions would disappear." If ethics replaced politics as the centerpiece of curriculum studies, we would teach what knowledge is of most worth, not that which promises the greatest return on our investment, whether economic or social or cognitive.

5   "Education as archival text," Marla Morris (2006, 76) points out, "is an active engagement with digging—digging through one's multifaceted registers of self-understanding—ironically through studying the lives of others." In addition to these instances—Woodson and Garvey—there are many more in the contemporary field: see, for instance Salvio 2007; Crocco, Munro and Weiler 1999. There is a resonance between Morris' notion of education as "archival" and Fidyk's (2010, 442) idea of "ancestral." Absent of any obvious links to "self-understanding" (central in Morris' idea), however, is Dimitriadis' (2010, 465) juxtaposition of Jean-Paul Sartre and Edward Said. Also missing in his chapter are any links to the intellectual history of the US field, as Sartre—*Nausea* in particular (see Dimitriadis 2010, 471)—was central to the work of Madeleine Grumet (see 1978). In his response to the chapter, Tom Barone kindly ignores Dimitradis' evident ignorance of Barone's own referencing of Sartre (see, for instance, Barone 2000, 230–239), saying simply (and diplomatically) that "Like Dimitriadis, I too have found inspiration in the works of Sartre and Said."

6   Gender and race also meet in Anthony L. Brown's (2011) revealing research on images of black males in the social sciences.

7   Even these fields could be reconceptualized if formulated through the lens of curriculum theory: see Handa 2011.

8   "This prime myth of the soul's connection with love, Psyche with Eros," Mary Aswell Doll (2011, 74) reminds, "turns discussion away from the grand gesture toward a process of seeing through, seeing in to the inwardness of things."

9   "Neoliberalism," Grimmett and Young (2012, 51) point out, "creates the environment in which people tend to defer to fate and accept their current circumstances as the upper limit of possibility." Like McKnight, if in different terms, Grimmett and Young (2012, 51) also emphasize activism in this

DOI: 10.1057/9781137303424

instance "talking back" to policy-makers: "The purpose here would be to revision a sense of agency that interrupts a fatalistic view of teaching and teacher education as mere pawn in the neo-liberalist policy juggernaut. This would not mean being naïve about the structural impediments to agency but it would involve fighting the tendency to see teacher education programs as victims of policy. Teacher educators would therefore have to reject passivity and engage the struggle to re-vision the work so that their practice is theoretically sensitive and grounded in moral purpose. They would have to work to sustain teacher education in a manner that spawns resilience within and among all practitioner ranks." Resilience comes not from "resistance," but, as they point out, from "moral purpose." While hardly abandoning the political, Grimmett and Young recognize it is by itself not enough; politics must be informed by ethics.

10   For John Weaver (2010, 191), the "posthuman condition reshapes human subjectivity, social justice, and human dignity." He uses the term "posthuman" because "it is the best term to capture the diversity and complexity of the intersection between humans and technology since the 1980s" (2010, 193). Supplementing the concept of "cyborg" with fyborg ("any bodily enhancement/transformation through any temporary technological intrusion into the body" [2010, 193]), Weaver (2010, 194) worries that the human body will lose its "materiality."

11   "[W]ithout a complex conception of love as a meaningful experience that contains what experience cannot master," Deborah Britzman (2006, 63) explains, "there is no way of understanding our inner world and its passionate currents." "Ethics," Britzman (2000, 33) writes, "accompanies the 'crafting' of memory and working through loss." It is our capacity to think through "instinctual conflict" and our relation to "reality" that allows us to formulate our sense of "ethical responsibility" (Britzman 2006, 50). That responsibility can be expressed, at least in part, through "hospitality" that Molly Quinn (2010, 101) positions as "central to the work of education." For Quinn (2010, 104), hospitality communicates love in a spiritual sense (see also Edgerton 1996, 64), and sometimes through "laughter" (2010, 108), enabling "healing" (2010, 109). None of these concepts shows up in Snaza's definitional formulae.

12   Baker (2009b, xxvi) reminds us of the "narcissism and prejudice that have been so central to the idea of community," as well as its reliance on the non-rational for organizing its "rationalized groupings."

13   Ferneding (2010, 179–183) does reference Macdonald as well as Huebner.

14   Ferneding references McLuhan (2010, 174) and Innis (2010, 176).

15   Referencing ancient Thai concepts of "space," Baker (2009, xix) points out that the concept of space is not universal, that "there was not simply one way to represent the world but rather that there was more than one world,

DOI: 10.1057/9781137303424

more than one imaginal domain." Premodern mapping methods in South East Asia, she continues, were not devoted to locating specific sites within a larger whole. Indeed, Baker (2009, xx) shows that the modern map is an "indispensable mediator" in "conceptualizing such macrospace as though it is a totality, a function that none of the premodern maps never performed." The very tendency toward totalization that accompanied the acceptance of power, identity, and discourse in the US field is at times reinscribed in the contemporary concept of "space." For Robert Helfenbein (2010, 306, emphasis added), "space constructed through discursive, interpretive, lived, and imagined practices *becomes* place." This assertion seems to acknowledge that history, culture, and lived experience structure a place, but does not the particularity of place disappear in the assertion that "space is everywhere" (Helfenbein 2010, 308)? The notion of "third space" (see Wang 2004) Helfenbein (2010, 309) depicts as "those spaces that speak, those spaces that lead and those spaces of possibility." That last concept suggests the reinstallation of "agency" (2010, 314), a concept Lisa Cary (2006, 135) never uses but which seems implied in her assertion of "an ethical turn toward responsibility in research."

16   "Students are reading in new ways," Mary Aswell Doll (2011, 50) suggests, "concentrating on image rather than narration.... They must halt, stop, make haste slowly (an alchemical slogan) if they are to attend to the other of the image. Of course, this is a different rhythm from what cyberspace demands.... The speed of the cyber world has made its junkies jumpy." But, Doll (2011, 50) points out, "the two rhythms need not be oppositional."

17   As John Weaver (2010, 192) appreciates: "There is no other field within education that is more artistic than curriculum theory." Arts-based research has become influential during the "next moment" and it, too, is registered in the Malewski *Handbook* (see Carpenter and Tavin 2010) as well as in recent work by Tom Barone and Elliot Eisner (2012) and Margaret Latta (in press). In Canada, a/r/t/ography studies the relations among artist-researcher-teacher (see Irwin and de Cosson 2004; Springgay et al. 2008).

18   The great political economist and communications theorist also drew upon his experience teaching in one-room rural schools in Norwich, Ontario, and Landonville, Alberta (Watson 2007, 16). As a "marginal intellectual" Innis came to believe that "an individual from the periphery could sustain intense cultural training leading to an indigenous critical perspective without consequent deracination" (2007, 17). See also Pinar 2011a, 163 n. 29.

19   "In the Hegelian-Marxian tradition, and in Freire's critical pedagogy," Dennis Carlson (2010, 203) points out, "part of what it means to become fully self-conscious is to recognize that we play an active role in producing culture and self." That "active role"—agency—was what was lost in the primacy of politics over ethics in US curriculum studies.

DOI: 10.1057/9781137303424

20   Complicating the concept of "creative solidarity," Janet L. Miller (2010, 97)
      writes: "nor do I think that 'we' can aim for one unitary version of 'creative
      solidarity." She continues: "So, how might we take up the challenges of
      difference, wherein static conceptions of 'identity' or isolated cultures and
      educational practices cannot function as refuge, within a concept of creative
      solidarity?" (2010, 97).

DOI: 10.1057/9781137303424

Epilogue

Abstract: *I point to the two intellectually "repressed" traditions in the field, specifically Jewish and international studies, whose articulation now can structure the reconceptualization of curriculum studies in the United States. From the former I take the model of Torah study that John Willinsky and Alan A. Block summarize, in which centuries of commentary comprise complicated conversation concerning the formation of ethical communities. From the latter I take the Brazilian concept of "enunciation," the Mexican sense of "polysemic," and the notion of "translation" in curriculum studies in South Africa to specify the significance of "place"—and its study in dialogical encounter with colleagues worldwide—as structuring efforts to formulate new concepts in the United States. In the field that is now unfolding, ethics may replace politics as the central concept in the field, restoring agency while reconstructing the concepts American scholars have been bequeathed. To illustrate, I conclude with Hongyu Wang's juxtaposition of "East" and "West" in her reconsideration of the concept of reconceptualization, emphasizing its recursive and regenerative elements.*

Pinar, F. William. *Curriculum Studies in the United States: Present Circumstances, Intellectual Histories.* New York: Palgrave Macmillan, 2013. DOI: 10.1057/9781137303424.

> Let's be a queer family with a different relation to generations.
>
> Patti Lather (2010, 75)

"What then can it mean," Jennifer Gilbert (2010, 65) asks, "to speak of a new generation[1] of curriculum theorists?" She wonders which concepts must be "destroyed" in the construction of "new objects of inquiry" and "avenues for thought?" How will vanquished objects and ideas, now "forgotten," return to "haunt" the new? Must "reconceptualization" and intellectual breakthrough involve aggression? That last question is mine, not Gilbert's, but I share her suspicion that disciplinary demands for "innovation" and "transformative practices" threaten aggression. Do these tendencies toward disciplinary violence—aggravated in times of "crisis"—invite repetition, not reconstruction?

Gilbert turns to psychoanalysis to underscore the fact that like the repressed more generally, violence returns, however academicians insist that they have expelled it from their disciplines in the names of rationality, research, and discovery. Gilbert reminds us that knowledge can occur through violence, and that violence originates within the subject as well as across society (2010, 65–66). The question of origins is crucial. Knowing the genesis of present circumstances not only contextualizes those circumstances but supports their surpassing. Institutionalized as disciplinary intellectual history, remembrance renders present circumstances "present" by situating them in the past. The parallel with psychoanalysis is not incidental.

"Ideas do not float freely among people," Charles David Axelrod (1979, 2–3) emphasizes, "they become rooted in commitments, ossified and sustained within intellectual communities; they are cradled among avid sponsors and defenders whose work relies on their stability." In US curriculum studies, it seems that scholars can be over-aware of ideas' "sponsors" and "defenders." Sometimes it seems that US curriculum studies is as much a social club as it is an academic discipline, with personal animosities and loyalties as important as scholarship itself in the consideration of concepts. With such intersubjective "infrastructure," concepts can remain long after their vibrancy has disappeared into citation without substance, name-dropping rather than reference. The institutionalization of such practices spells disciplinary stasis. "Intellectual breakthrough," Axelrod (1979, 10) cautions, "represents works whose

DOI: 10.1057/9781137303424

relation to the community changes and can actually betray itself in the process of its own institutionalization."

How? Organized around institutional and personal alliances, the "community" of scholars, Axelrod (1979, 10) argues, "hides the dialectical momentum of founding works and celebrates their concrete reproduction." Rather than engaging in that subjective threading intellectual craftsmanship requires, we succumb to mechanical reproduction. Through reproduction of once-novel ideas—power, discourse, identity—the community of scholars "obscures the difference between the original and the copy, between the critical and the obedient" (1979, 10). When widely accepted, concepts become dereferentialized. They fade into the background, assumptions needing no specification. Disciplinary advancement depends on intellectual innovation within an ongoing conversation, and that innovation cannot occur unless scholars recognize, in their close and critical attention to present circumstances, that new concepts must address the extra-discursive, that sphere of the lived that is not yet thought or spoken. Concepts' non-coincidence with themselves reflects, in Radhakrishnan's phrasing (2008, 39) "the always already historicality of the present."

The project of psychoanalysis—and of the intellectual advancement of curriculum studies—requires reorienting scholarship so that it stays attuned to its source. Read metaphorically, Axelrod (1979, 25) argues, Freud's agenda can be interpreted as an effort to return science to an immediate relationship with its source, to become "faithful to itself." In our case, this is a call to become faithful to educational experience through academic study, engaged in complicated conversation in solitude and assembly. In Freud's psychoanalysis, Axelrod (1979, 25) reminds, there are regular appeals to the question of genesis, evident in the constancy of the concept of "primal." The term "primal" is interesting, Axelrod (1979, 25) points out, as it denotes that which is "first, most significant, and essential." Freud's preoccupation with genesis communicates his concerns for significance and essence (1979, 25). It is the past we must reactivate in the present to decipher the meaning of what we undergo now. As Erik Malewski (2010, 37) summarizes:

> Flux and change, hybrid spaces, reading differently, divergent perspectives, different contexts, status questions, and unstudied histories, the intent is to move the curriculum field in multiple directions with the hope that more compelling and beneficial ways of knowing will begin to appear.

DOI: 10.1057/9781137303424

Within this disciplinary complexity, remaining focused on origins—reiterating amidst shifting circumstances the canonical-curriculum question *what knowledge is of most worth?*—can act as a rudder, providing disciplinary continuity and enabling disciplinary innovation. It can also reanimate the field by regularly returning us to that experienced reality our concepts cannot yet comprehend, what is repressed in what we assume to be true now. What was repressed in the primacy of politics in the US field? The short answer is *ethics.*

Ethics may replace politics as curriculum studies' primary category. That has already occurred in the important work of Alan A. Block (2007, 2009), scholarship which names the repression of ethical—and specifically Jewish thought in US curriculum studies with its uncritical adoration of progressivism, a secular form of Christianity (Tröhler 2006, 2011) that positions progress as primary. Reproduction and resistance theory reinscribed the dialectic of damnation and salvation through good works structuring the eschatology of Christianity. Teaching became inflated as the secular form of testifying to the "afterlife," e.g. schools as laboratories of democracy reconstructing society, affirming the historical inevitability of democracy. The curriculum question—*what knowledge is of most worth?*—devolved first into instrumentality: how do we get from here to there? Method substituted for substance, but the worst was yet to come, as the failure of social engineering and the triumph of capitalism in education spelled an endemic cynicism we called politics. Everything was political we complained, and with that "realism" the curriculum question reached its vulgar bottom. No longer could we ask *what* knowledge is of most worth, as all knowledge was "always already" tainted by its political character. Instead, the politically preoccupied only wanted to know "*whose* knowledge is of most worth?" (see Pinar 2009, 148, n. 3)

In Alan Block's *oevure*—which began in Marxism (1992)—the collective and the historical remain but are now sacralized as reverence for both humanity and history. Politics remains but is now subservient to ethics. Teaching is no longer triumphant; it becomes the servant of study. "Study," Block (2004, 2) asserts simply but powerfully, "like prayer, is a way of being—it is an ethics." While not new (see Tom 1984), ethics' time may have come when in popular culture virtuality substitutes for actuality. In such circumstances it may be time to juxtapose the fluid and contingent with more enduring forms of engagement, including those associated with Jewish traditions of thought (see Block 2004; Morris 2001, 2006).[2] As expressions of embodied subjectivity in the world,

DOI: 10.1057/9781137303424

ethics restructures social relations away from the cynicism an exclusively political perspective compels, to one focused on what is ethically right in specific situations. From being impaled as passive on a never-ending wheel of reproduction and resistance—identity and discourse replaced power but the dereferentialized dynamic remained the same—ethics repositions us within the eventfulness of the quotidian.

John Willinsky provides a succinct summary of how Jewish traditions can reconceptualize our conception of curriculum and of curriculum studies, installing, as Block has argued, the primacy of study. Willinsky (2006, 162) tells us that Jewish scholars began recording the oral rabbinic commentaries on the Torah, known as *midrash*, at least as early as the second century BC, when Rabbi Judah HaNasi edited the oral legal commentaries. Block (2004, 21) summarizes this ongoing complicated conversation: "Talmud is a way of thinking about how to live in the world based upon an ethical ontology." What is that "way of thinking?"

The rabbis[3], Willinsky (2006, 162) reminds, were providing "links from this sacred text to various interpretations that introduced mythic elements, related biblical verses ("As it is said…"), and related materials." Derived from the Hebrew root for *to seek out* or *to inquire*, Willinsky (2006, 162) explains, midrash "surrounds, in effect, a core text in a continuing spiral of context and connection." "That is," Block (2004, 60) tells us, "Talmudic discussion does not arrive at a final and definitive decision, so much as explore the alternative positions presented."[4] In different terms these quoted passages communicate what I am affirming with "horizontality" and "verticality," namely the ethical obligation that informs our academic study and pedagogical participation in an ongoing disciplinary conversation that is in its conceptual structure dialogic and temporal. Whatever the "core" text—even that of the evidently eugenicist Bobbitt—our professional ethics requires us to address it (as Winfield has done), to situate our contribution in an ongoing stream of "commentary, context, and connection" that inevitably incurs its reconstruction.[5]

When midrash was printed in book form, Willinsky (2006, 162–163) continues, the text was centered on the page, "surrounded by blocks of Hebrew text" comprised of commentaries, "interpretations, logical reasoning, disagreements, and cross-references, whether by rabbinic luminaries of ancient times or more modern figures." The entirety of these constitutes the Talmud (Block 2004, 62–63). One important consequence, Willinsky (2006, 163) suggests, is that "although any one commentary is at once authoritative in its declarations on the page, it

DOI: 10.1057/9781137303424

sits within a rich context of vying commentaries, inviting only further interpretation and judgment." In this particular and provocative sense, curriculum and curriculum studies—as complicated conversation—are secular academic versions of Talmud:

> Readings are layers on readings, suggesting provisional senses of meaning within possibilities of further contextualization. In the very way that midrash is laid out on the page, it make clear how knowledge—in the form of understandings, interpretations, and connections—moves among minds and how various forms of knowledge work on teach other. (Willinsky 2006, 163)

Here Willinsky (2006, 163) is thinking of "how knowledge is shaped by the very layout or design of the page and this strikes me as worth keeping in mind in thinking about the design of publishing environments for online journals." Perhaps inadvertently, Willinsky has also presented a disciplinary model of how academic fields can remain animated by attunement to their sources as they institutionalize their ongoing obligation to understand present circumstances. It is a succinct statement of the intersection between intellectual histories and present circumstances.

That intersection is also evident in Hongyu Wang's chapter in the 2010 *Handbook*, wherein she gestures toward a cross-cultural understanding of the next moment of US curriculum studies by juxtaposing Kristeva's concept of "intimate revolt" with Laozi's conception of yin/yang (2010, 374). That juxtaposition, Wang (2010, 374) suggests, might provide "multiple bridges" toward the "new generation's task." How? In Kristeva, Wang (2010, 375) explains, the etymology of the word *revolt* reveals "circular movement" and "temporal return" in its Latin antecedent. Wang notes that the political meaning of revolt—with its connotation of a complete and even violent break with the past—did not appear until modernity. In contrast to that sense of aggression and rupture, Kristeva, working psychoanalytically, locates revolt in oedipal tension and regression to the archaic (see Wang 2010, 375). "Facing the failure of rebellious ideologies (to march into a promised land) and the dominance of a consumer culture (in flattening the depth of psychic life)," Wang (2010, 375) explains, we must rethink "revolt," and Kristeva's formulation of it is more complex and subtle than what its vernacular political meaning implies. For Kristeva, revolt is not confined to social contestation but incorporates self-questioning, and "intimacy" that can "renew psychic space" (2010,

DOI: 10.1057/9781137303424

375). Translating into my terms, revolt becomes an engagement characterized less by abrasive confrontation than by an ongoing (on occasion even seductive) dialogical encounter. It can occur within solitary meditation as well as in public debate; in both settings the challenge becomes the exploration of intimacy, not the instigation of violence. "Revolt" is "open," "transformative," and "creative," Wang (2010, 375) explains, and it is "simultaneously" in the service of cultural, political, and psychic "working through" and "renaissance." Such "working through" and "renaissance" constitute subjective and social reconstruction.

Noting that "reversal" and "return" can be used "interchangeably" in the ancient Chinese language, Wang (2010, 375) reminds us that "everything" has its "opposite," and that opposites attract. But this is no confrontation of contraries, Wang notes (referencing here the *Tao Te Ching*), as "everything always changes towards its reversal" (2010, 375). Wang emphasizes this point: "A time of vigor leads to a time of decay; strength comes from holding onto softness; what is worn out will become renewed" (2010, 375). Sounding slightly like Freud for the moment, Wang (2010, 375) asserts that returning to the "original source of life—Tao as the way of nature—is the direction of movement." Such a recursive return to Tao—Wang (2010, 375) specifies its "emptiness, quietude, and harmony"—engenders "renewal" and "regeneration." As in psychoanalysis it seems, the Taoist conception of "change" assumes an "interconnected sense of the world in which one thing can become something else" (2010, 375). At this point Wang (2010, 376) returns us to curriculum studies: "*Is not curriculum—currere—about movement, moving out of the frozen state, moving toward what is yet to come?*" Indeed, it is.

This resemblance between autobiography and disciplinarity is reiterated in Wang's juxtaposition of "plural singularity" (derived from Kristeva's concept of intimate revolt) and "return" (derived from Taoism), enabling us to "embrace interdependence." Such interdependence is, Wang (2010, 381) suggests, a "childlike" state, not "dependency," but, rather, an "endless playful openness." Such playfulness, Wang (2010, 382) continues, reenacts "translation," a concept central to curriculum studies in South Africa (see Pinar 2010, 232, 234–238). Translation, Wang (2010, 382) explains, denotes dwelling in a "third space," characterized by "attentiveness to the other," but this does not disavow fidelity to oneself but, rather, the occasion for subjective reconstruction. While "difficult," this space of translation is "generative." Wang (2010, 383) suggests that translation can be an "exemplar" of a "creativity marked by cocreativity."

DOI: 10.1057/9781137303424

Does this space of translation return us to the challenges of "creative solidarity" in the formation of "communities without consensus?" This space is the site of internationalism.

In translating the curriculum, Wang (2010, 384) concludes, we create "intersections," and not only within the field but with other fields as well, and with those outside academe. It is at the "interstice" between the "exterior" and the "interior," she continues, that we may create a "parallel space"—curriculum as "revolt" (2010, 384). This interstice can be found, I suggest, between intellectual histories and present circumstances, and evident in the model of complicated conversation that the Talmud enacts. Located at the intersection of past with present, then, the challenge, as Wang (2010, 384) appreciates, is "not to highlight the cutting edge of a new generation but to confront the recursive nature of human problems that we are perpetually facing, with their own specific questions and issues contextualized in history, culture, place, and concrete personhood for our age." For me, the concept of allegory[6] summarizes this complexity as it denotes doubled consciousness. Such a consciousness—can it become a professional ethos for the next moment?—implies obligation to cultivate one's own creative singularity through engagement with others in reactivating the past repressed in the present. That past is not only the intellectual history of the curriculum field but also what was repressed in the US national past: Judaism and internationalism, themselves intertwined historically and politically.[7]

With its promise of distantiation from the provincial, such internationalization can be cosmopolitan in its consequences, enabling us to reconstruct how we think about present circumstances and their histories. Through concepts simultaneously old and new we can devise locally inflected forms of "agency." Intellectual engagement is what is reactivated through enunciation of the eventfulness that is the quotidian. Through ongoing academic study and democratically structured dialogue with colleagues everywhere we form a "single fund of world invention" (Feenberg 2010, 111). In doing so we convert the discredited concept of "objectives" into the "great cause" the field of curriculum studies creates and represents (Pinar 2011d, 236). Not only an academic field, this cause is the curriculum itself, that ancient ongoing complicated conversation in which we are called to participate.

Through intellectual labor we can reconstruct internationalism as we struggle to understand our present circumstances and the concepts we have been bequeathed. In this essay I have suggested that the legacy of

DOI: 10.1057/9781137303424

Christianity—specifically its secular form known as "progressivism"—constrains US-based scholars' capacity to preserve the very meaning of education—and the informed agency education engenders—amidst crushing political circumstances. Remembering the history of the crucial conversation in which we are engaged—construing the academic discipline as a secular version of Talmud—can steady us in this nightmare time, can prompt us to reformulate the concepts by which the curriculum can be understood, reconstructing the canon as we encounter the return of the repressed. "Intimate revolt"—with its recursive return of the past enabling the surpassing of the present—authenticates the disciplinary speech political repression silenced. Sustained academic study of our intellectual histories and attuned analyses of present circumstances promises to precipitate a second reconceptualization of curriculum studies in the United States.

Notes

1   As will Hongyu Wang (whose chapter I will discuss momentarily), Erik Malewski (2010, xiii) contests "the notion of generations of curriculum scholars [as] either wholly rebelling against the previous generation or wholly writing in their shadows." Focused upon conversation, Malewski (2010, xiii) disputes any "claim to post-reconceptualization as the terrain of a younger generation."

2   Block (2004, 10) points out that "[t]he field of curriculum has been forever dominated by the discourses derived from Greek, Roman, and Christian principles and by practices and methods that derive from those principles" (see also Block 2004, 20, 21, 27.) Schwab is Block's searing example, arguing persuasively that "Schwab's work *in* curriculum, and particularly his exploration *of* curriculum in the four seminal essays that appeared between 1969 and 1984, have been interpreted within the framework of these Greek, Roman, and Christian discourse systems and have been, therefore, either misinterpreted or misunderstood—perhaps even as a result of Schwab's own reticence to name the 'J' word in his published work" (Block 2004, 15). Understood in Jewish terms, Schwab's conception of "deliberation" becomes incalculably more rich than deciphered through Christian or secularized terms. "Schwab's deliberation," Block (2004, 17) writes, "seems to me to mirror Talmudic practice." Evidently Ralph Tyler, in 1973 at least, thought Jewish intellectuality was best confined to Jewish schools (see Block 2004, 49). And "the preparation of objectives" (Tyler's [1949] first "principle"), Block (2004, 54) notes, "was not what Schwab had in mind." Does the emphasis of the

DOI: 10.1057/9781137303424

US field upon teaching rather than study disclose its Christian rather than Jewish bias?

3   Block (2009, 89) writes, "the Rabbis have placed education as the central determinant of holiness." He adds, significantly: "Education is our means out of the desert. While we study, there is no desert. And this study built upon faith is the substance of curriculum" (Block 2009, 111).

4   "Not a Socratic monologue," Block (2004, 61) explains, "Talmudic discourse is critical inquiry often digressing far from the original topic." Such digression has spiritual significance. Block quotes Halbertal and Halbertal (1998, 459): "The unique conversational structure of education in the Yeshiva and its attempt at maximizing cross-generational exchange aims at shaping the study of the text of Torah as a communal experience. Moreover, study is institutionalized in the Beit Midrash as a performative act carried out by the students' participations. In such a discursive model, students are not passive spectators in a reality shaped by teachers. A *Beit Midrash* is a learning space shaped by the intensity and quality of the ongoing exchange of its students." "Literally," Block (2004, 61) explains in footnote 2, "this Hebrew phrase means 'house of study.'"

5   If the contemporary US field is, as Malewski (2010, xv, n. 2) depicts it, "chaotic, layered, and discontinuous,... more of a mosaic than a linear line of progression," then the discipline disappears. As Willinsky's summary of midrash shows, "mosaic" and "layered" are laudable precisely because they correct for the "chaotic" and "discontinuous," underscoring the temporal continuity of past and present.

6   In her response to Wang's chapter, Xin Li (2010, 387) references the legendary Canadian scholar Northrop Frye who underlined "the figurative use of the term resonance and emphasized its capacity for stretching images over time and bridging temporal distance in a manner metaphorically, of flying away from the original as well as maintaining some elements." This states succinctly the concept of allegory (Pinar 2012, 54–62).

7   Recall that internationalism and Judaism were linked in the minds of anti-Semites who condemned as "rootless cosmopolitans" (Appiah 2006, xvi). One is reminded of Paraskeva's conception of an "itinerant curriculum theory," but one that "disrespects" the canon by reconstructing it in intimate (e.g. knowing and dialogic) revolt.

DOI: 10.1057/9781137303424

References

Abbs, Peter. 1974. *Autobiography in Education: An Introduction to the Subjective Discipline of Autobiography and its Central Place in the Education of Teachers.* London: Heinemann.

Amariglio, Jack, Resnick, Stephen, and Wolff, Richard D. 1993. Division and Difference in the "Discipline" of Economics. In *Knowledges: Historical and Critical Studies in Disciplinarity* edited by Ellen Messer-Davidow, David R. Shumway, and David J. Sylvan (150–184). Charlottesville: University Press of Virginia.

Anderson, Amanda and Valente, Joseph (eds). 2002. *Disciplinarity at the Fin de Siècle.* Princeton, New Jersey: Princeton University Press.

Appelbaum, Peter. 2010. Response to Alberto J. Rodriguez: Let's Do Lunch. In *Curriculum Studies Handbook: The Next Moment,* edited by Erik Malewski (460–463). New York: Routledge.

Appiah, Kwame Anthony. 2006. *Cosmopolitanism: Ethics in a World of Strangers.* New York: Norton.

Asher, Nina. 2010. Decolonizing Curriculum. In *Curriculum Studies Handbook: The Next Moment,* edited by Erik Malewski (393–402). New York: Routledge.

Associated Press. 2012, March 20. Panel Says School's Failings Could Threaten Economy and National Security. *The New York Times* Vol. CLXI (55,716), A12.

Association for Supervision and Curriculum Development. 1962. *Perceiving, Behaving, Becoming: A New Focus for Education.* Washington, DC: ASCD.

Axelrod, Charles David. 1979. *Studies in Intellectual Breakthrough*. Amherst: University of Massachusetts Press.

Baker, Al. 2012, July 30. Certifying Teachers, More by How They Teach Than How They Test. *The New York Times* CLXI (55, 848), A1, A3.

Baker, Bernadette M. 2001. *In Perpetual Motion: Theories of Power, Educational History, and the Child*. New York: Peter Lang.

Baker, Bernadette M. 2002. The Hunt for Disability: The New Eugenics and the Normalization of Schoolchildren. *Teachers College Record*, 104: 663–703.

Baker, Bernadette (ed.). 2009. *New Curriculum History*. Rotterdam: Sense Publishers.

Baker, Bernadette M. 2010. The Unconscious of History? Mesmerism and the Production of Scientific Objects for Curriculum Historical Research. In *Curriculum Studies Handbook: The Next Moment*, edited by Erik Malewski (341–364). New York: Routledge.

Banchero, Stephanie. 2011, December 1. Teacher Faction Expands to L.A. *The Wall Street Journal*, Vol. CCLVIII (No. 129), A6.

Banchero, Stephanie. 2012, February 13. Bills Prod Schools to Hold Back Third-Graders. *The Wall Street Journal*, Vol. CCLIX (No. 35), A3.

Banchero, Stephanie. 2012, February 15. Plan Offers $5 Billion To Improve Teaching. *The Wall Street Journal*, Vol. CCLIX (No. 37), A3.

Banchero, Stephanie. 2012, March 8. Teacher Evaluations Pose Test for States. *The Wall Street Journal*, Vol. CCLIX (No. 5), A2.

Banchero, Stephanie and Simon, Stephanie. 2011, November 12–13. My Teacher is an App. *The Wall Street Journal*, Vol. CCLVIII (No. 14), C1-C2.

Barone, Tom. 2000. Aesthetics, Politics, and Educational Inquiry. New York: Peter Lang.

Barone, Thomas. 2010. Response to Greg Dimitriadis: The Curriculum Scholar as Socially Committed Provocateur: Extending the Ideas of Said, Sartre, and Dimitriadis. In *Curriculum Studies Handbook: The Next Moment*, edited by Erik Malewski (477–480). New York: Routledge.

Barone, Tom and Eisner, Elliot W. 2012. *Arts Based Research*. Thousand Oaks, California: Sage.

Beck, Ulrich. 2009. *World at Risk*. Malden, Massachusetts: Polity.

Berger, Joseph. 2012, February 25. Resilient Students Awarded Times Scholarships. *The New York Times* Vol. CLXI (55,692), A16.

DOI: 10.1057/9781137303424

Berliner, David C. and Biddle, Bruce J. 1995. *The Manufactured Crisis: Myths, Fraud, and the Attack on America's Public Schools*. Cambridge, Massachusetts: Perseus.

Berry, Theodora Regina. 2010. Response to LaVada Brandon: Honoring Our Founders, Respecting Our Contemporaries: In the Words of a Critical Race Feminist Curriculum Theorist. In *Curriculum Studies Handbook: The Next Moment*, edited by Erik Malewski (138–141). New York: Routledge.

Block, Alan A. 1992. *Anonymous Toil: A Re-Evaluation of the American Radical Novel in the Twentieth Century*. Lanham, Maryland: University Press of America.

Block, Alan A. 2004. *Talmud, Curriculum, and the Practical*. New York: Peter Lang.

Block, Alan A. 2007. *Pedagogy, Religion, and Practice: Reflections on Ethics and Teaching*. New York: Palgrave Macmillan.

Block, Alan A. 2009. *Ethics and Teaching: A Religious Perspective on Revitalizing Education*. New York: Palgrave Macmillan.

Block, Alan A. 2010. And They'll Say That It's a Movement. In *Curriculum Studies Handbook: The Next Moment*, edited by Erik Malewski (523–527). New York: Routledge.

Bobbitt, Franklin. 1918. *The Curriculum*. Boston: Houghton Mifflin.

Bohm, David. 1996. *On Dialogue*. London: Routledge.

Bowers, C. A. 1995. *Educating for an Ecologically Sustainable Culture*. Albany: State University of New York Press.

Bowers, C. A. 2000. *Let Them Eat Data*. Athens: University of Georgia Press.

Bowers, C. A. 2001. *Educating for Eco-Justice and Community*. Athens: University of Georgia Press.

Bowers, C. A. 2005. *The False Promises of Constructivist Theories of Learning. A Global and Ecological Critique*. New York: Peter Lang.

Brandon, LaVada. 2010. Remembering Carter Woodson (1875–1950). In *Curriculum Studies Handbook: The Next Moment*, edited by Erik Malewski (125–137). New York: Routledge.

Britzman, Deborah P. 2006. *Novel Education: Psychoanalytic Studies of Learning and Not Learning*. New York: Peter Lang.

Brooks, Nancy J. 2010. Response to Karen Ferneding: Smashing the Feet of Idols: Curriculum Phronesis as a Way through the Wall. In *Curriculum Studies Handbook: The Next Moment*, edited by Erik Malewski (185–189). New York: Routledge.

DOI: 10.1057/9781137303424

Brown, Anthony L. 2011. "Same Old Stories": The Black Male in Social Science and Educational Literarure, 1930s to the Present. *Teachers College Record* 113 (9), 2047–2079.

Burke, Kevin J. 2011. *Masculinities and Other Hopeless Causes at an All-Boys Catholic School.* New York: Peter Lang.

Carlson, Dennis. 2010. Response to John A. Weaver: Questioning Technology: Heidegger, Haraway, and Democratic Education. In *Curriculum Studies Handbook: The Next Moment*, edited by Erik Malewski (201–205). New York: Routledge.

Carpenter II, B. Stephen and Tavin, Kevin. 2010. Art Education Beyond Reconceptualization: Enacting Curriculum Through/With/By/For/ Of/In/Beyond/As Visual Culture, Community, and Public Pedagogy. In *Curriculum Studies Handbook: The Next Moment*, edited by Erik Malewski (244–258). New York: Routledge.

Cary, Lisa J. 2006. *Curriculum Spaces: Discourse, Postmodernism, and Educational Research.* New York: Peter Lang.

Casemore, Brian. 2008. *The Autobiographical Demand of Place. Curriculum Inquiry in the American South.* New York: Peter Lang.

Casselman, Ben. 2012, January 9. Economists Set Rules on Ethics. *The Wall Street Journal*, Vol. CCLIX (No. 6), A2.

Chauncey, George. 2000. The Queer History and Politics of Lesbian and Gay Studies. In *Queer Frontiers: Millennial Geographies, Genders, and Generations*, edited by Joseph A. Boone, Martin Dupuis, Martin Meeker, Karin Quimby, Cindy Sarver, Debra Silverman, and Rosemary Weatherston (298–315). Madison: University of Wisconsin Press.

Christian, William. 1996. *George Grant: A Biography.* Toronto: University of Toronto Press.

Chow, Rey. 2002. Theory, Area Studies, Cultural Studies: Issues of Pedagogy in Multiculturalism. In *Learning Places: The Afterlives of Area Studies* edited by Masao Miyoshi and D. H. Harootunian (103–118). Durham, North Carolina: Duke University Press.

Chozick, Amy. 2012, July 24. News Corp. Brands Unit for Education as Amplify. *The New York Times* CLXI (55, 842), B3.

Christian, William. 1996. *George Grant: A Biography.* Toronto: University of Toronto Press.

Coyle, Diane. 2007. *The Soulful Science: What Economists Really Do and Why It Matters.* Princeton, New Jersey: Princeton University Press.

DOI: 10.1057/9781137303424

Crocco, Margaret Smith, Munro, Petra, and Weiler, Kathleen. 1999. *Pedagogies of Resistance: Women Educator Activists, 1880–1960*. [Foreword by Nel Noddings.] New York: Teachers College Press.

Davis, Brent. 2004. *Inventions of Teaching: A Genealogy*. Mahwah, New Jersey: Lawrence Erlbaum.

Davis, Brent, Sumara, Dennis, and Luce-Kapler, Rebecca. 2000. *Engaging Minds*. Mahwah, New Jersey: Lawrence Erlbaum.

De Castell, Suzanne and Jenson, Jennifer. 2003. Serious Play. Curriculum for a Post-Talk Era. *Journal of the Canadian Association for Curriculum Studies* 1 (1), 47–52.

Delbanco, Andrew. 2012, March 9. A Smug Education? *The New York Times* Vol. CLXI (55,705), A21.

Deleuze, Gilles. 1993. *The Fold: Leibniz and the Baroque*. [Forward and translation by T. Conley.] Minneapolis and London: University of Minnesota Press.

Deleuze, Gilles and Guattari, Félix. 1987. *A Thousand Plateaus: Capitalism and Schizophrenia*. [Foreword and translation by Brian Massumi.] Minneapolis: University of Minnesota Press.

Deming, David. 2012, February 1. What I Learned From a Brainiac. *The Wall Street Journal*, Vol. CCLIX (No. 25), A15.

Dillon, Sam. 2011, December 15. Failure Rate of Schools Overstated, Study Says. *The New York Times* Vol. CLXI (55, 620), A1, A28.

Dimitriadis, Greg. 2010. Edward Said and Jean-Paul Sartre: Critical Modes of Intellectual Life. In *Curriculum Studies Handbook: The Next Moment*, edited by Erik Malewski (464–476). New York: Routledge.

Doll, Mary Aswell. 2011. *The More of Myth. A Pedagogy of Diversion*. Rotterdam: Sense Publishers.

Doll, Jr., William E. 1993. *A Post-Modern Perspective on Curriculum*. New York: Teachers College Press.

Doll, Jr., William E. 1998. Curriculum and Concepts of Control. [Assisted by Al Alcazar.] In *Curriculum: Toward New Identities* edited by William F. Pinar (295–323). New York: Garland.

Doll, Jr., William E. 2004. Ghosts and the Curriculum. In *Curriculum Visions* edited by William E. Doll, Jr. and Noel Gough (23–70). New York: Peter Lang.

Doll, Jr., William E. 2005. The Culture of Method. In *Chaos, Complexity, Curriculum, and Culture*, edited by William E. Doll, Jr., M. Jayne Fleener, Donna Trueit, and John St. Julien (21–75). New York: Peter Lang.

DOI: 10.1057/9781137303424

Doll, Jr., William E., Fleener, M. Jayne, Trueit, Donna, and St. Julien, John (eds). 2005. *Chaos, Complexity, Curriculum, and Culture*. New York: Peter Lang.

Edgerton, Susan Huddleston. 1996. *Translating the Curriculum: Multiculturalism into Cultural Studies*. New York: Routledge.

Feenberg, Andrew. 2010. *Between Reason and Experience. Essays in Technology and Modernity*. Foreword by Brian Wynee. Afterword by Michel Callon. Cambridge, Massachusetts: MIT Press.

Fernandez, Manny. 2012, April 9. At Texas Schools, Making Do on a Shoestring: Walks Are Long and Staffs Are Short as State Budget Cuts Force Changes. *The New York Times* Vol. CLXI (55,736), A10.

Ferneding, Karen. 2010. Understanding Curriculum Studies in the Space of Technological Flow. In *Curriculum Studies Handbook: The Next Moment*, edited by Erik Malewski (171–184). New York: Routledge.

Fidyk, Alexandra. 2010. Response to Erik Malewski and Teresa Rishel: "Invisible Loyalty": Approaching Suicide From a Web of Relations. In *Curriculum Studies Handbook: The Next Moment*, edited by Erik Malewski (439–444). New York: Routledge.

Foster, Thomas. 2005. *The Souls of Cyberfolk: Posthumanism as Vernacular Theory*. Minneapolis: University of Minnesota Press.

Fuller, Steve. 1993. Disciplinary Boundaries and the Rhetoric of the Social Sciences. In *Knowledges: Historical and Critical Studies in Disciplinarity* edited by Ellen Messer-Davidow, David R. Shumway, and David J. Sylvan (125–149). Charlottesville: University Press of Virginia.

Gates, Jr., Henry Louis. 1990. Critical Remarks. In *Anatomy of Racism*, edited by David Theo Goldberg (319–329). Minneapolis: University of Minnesota Press.

Gaztambide-Fernández, Rubén A. 2010. Toward Creative Solidarity in the "Next" Moment of Curriculum Work. In *Curriculum Studies Handbook: The Next Moment*, edited by Erik Malewski (78–95). New York: Routledge.

Gershon, Walter S. 2011. Introduction: Towards a Sensual Curriculum. *Journal of Curriculum Theorizing* 27 (2), 1–16.

Gilbert, Jennifer. 2010. Reading Histories: Curriculum Theory, Psychoanalysis, and Generational Violence. In *Curriculum Studies Handbook: The Next Moment*, edited by Erik Malewski (63–72). New York: Routledge.

DOI: 10.1057/9781137303424

Grimmett, Peter P. and Halvorson, Mark. 2010. From Understanding Curriculum to Creating Curriculum: The Case for the Co-Evolution of Re-Conceptualized Design with Re-Conceptualized Curriculum. *Curriculum Inquiry* 40 (2), 241–262.

Grimmett, Peter P. and Young, Jon C. 2012. *Teacher Certification and Professional Status of Teaching in North America. The New Battleground for Public Education.* Charlotte, North Carolina: Information Age Publishing.

Grande, Sandy. 2004. *Red Pedagogy: Native American Social and Political Thought.* Lanham, Maryland: Rowman & Littlefield.

Grumet, Madeleine R. 1978. Songs and Situations. In *Qualitative Evaluation* edite by George Willis (274–315), Berkeley, California: McCutchan.

Grumet, Madeleine R. 1988. *Bitter Milk: Women and Teaching.* Amherst: University of Massachusetts Press.

Grumet, Madeleine R. 2010. Response to Nina Asher: Subject Position and Subjectivity in Curriculum Theory. In *Curriculum Studies Handbook: The Next Moment*, edited by Erik Malewski (403–409). New York: Routledge.

Guillory, Nichole A. 2010. (A) Troubling Curriculum: Public Pedagogies of Black Women Rappers. In *Curriculum Studies Handbook: The Next Moment*, edited by Erik Malewski (209–222). New York: Routledge.

Halbertal, M. and Halbertal, T. H. 1998. The Yeshiva. In *Philosophers on Education*, edited by A. O. Rorty. New York: Routledge.

Hall, David L. 1994. *Richard Rorty: Prophet and Poet of the New Pragmatism.* Albany: State University of New York Press.

Halperin, David M. 2009. *What Do Gay Men Want? An Essay on Sex, Risk, and Subjectivity.* Ann Arbor: University of Michigan Press.

Hampton, Eber. 1995. Towards a Redefinition of Indian Education. In *First Nations Education in Canada: The Circle Unfolds* edited by Marie Battiste and Jean Barman (5–46). Vancouver: University of British Columbia Press.

Handa, Yuichi. 2011. What Does Understanding Mean for Teachers? Relationship as a Metaphor for Knowing. New York: Routledge.

Hansen, Emmanuel. 1977. *Frantz Fanon: Social and Political thought.* Columbus: Ohio State University Press.

Harvey, David. 2009. *Cosmopolitanism and the Geographies of Freedom.* New York: Columbia University Press.

DOI: 10.1057/9781137303424

Harvey, David. 2010. *The Enigma of Capital and the Crises of Capitalism.* New York: Oxford University Press.

Helfenbein, Robert J. 2010. Thinking through Scale: Critical Geography and Curriculum Spaces. In *Curriculum Studies Handbook: The Next Moment,* edited by Erik Malewski (304–317). New York: Routledge.

Henderson, James. 2010. Response to B. Stephen Carpenter II and Kevin Tavin: Sustaining Artistry and Leadership in Democratic Curriculum Work. In *Curriculum Studies Handbook: The Next Moment,* edited by Erik Malewski (259–262). New York: Routledge.

Henderson, J. and Kesson, K. 2003. *Curriculum Wisdom.* Upper Saddle River, New Jersey: Prentice-Hall.

Hendry, Petra Munro. 1999. Political Activism as Teaching: Jane Addams and Ida B. Wells. In *Pedagogies of Resistance: Women Educator Activists, 1880–1960* edited by Margaret Smith Crocco, Petra Munro and Kathleen Weiler (19–45). New York: Teachers College Press.

Hendry, Petra Munro. 2010. Response to Denise Taliaferro-Baszile: The Self: A Bricolage of Curricular Absence. In *Curriculum Studies Handbook: The Next Moment,* edited by Erik Malewski (496–499). New York: Routledge.

Hendry, Petra Munro. 2011. *Engendering Curriculum History.* New York: Routledge.

Hensley, Nathan 2011. *Curriculum Studies Gone Wild. Bioregional Education and the Scholarship of Sustainability.* New York: Peter Lang.

Howard, Adam. 2008. *Learning Privilege: Lessons of Power and Identity in Affluent Schooling.* New York: Routledge.

Howard, Adam and Tappan, Mark. 2010. Complicating the Social and Cultural Aspects of Social Class: Toward a Conception of Social Class as Identity. In *Curriculum Studies Handbook: The Next Moment,* edited by Erik Malewski (322–334). New York: Routledge.

Hu, Winnie. 2012, February 10. 10 States Are Given Waivers From Education Law. *The New York Times* Vol. CLXI (55,677), A13.

Hu, Winnie and Gebeloff, Robert. 2012, February 27. After Release of Teacher Ratings, A Focus on "Top" Teachers: Questions Remain About Validity of Data. *The New York Times* Vol. CLXI (55,694), A15.

Huebner, Dwayne. 1999. *The Lure of the Transcendent: Collected Essays.* [Edited by Vikki Hillis. Collected and introduced by William F. Pinar.] Mahwah, New Jersey: Lawrence Erlbaum.

DOI: 10.1057/9781137303424

Irwin, Rita L. and Alex de Cosson (eds). 2004. *A/r/tography: Rendering Self through Arts-based Living Inquiry*. Vancouver, British Columbia: Pacific Educational Press.

Jackson, Philip. 1968. *Life in Classrooms*. New York: Holt, Rinehart & Winston, Inc.

Jackson, Philip. 2012. *What Is Education?* Chicago: University of Chicago Press.

Jagose, Annamarie. 1996. *Queer Theory: An Introduction*. New York: New York University Press.

Jaramillo, Nathalia. 2010. Response to Nichole A. Guillory: The Politics of Patriarchal Discourse: A Feminist Rap. In *Curriculum Studies Handbook: The Next Moment*, edited by Erik Malewski (223–227). New York: Routledge.

Jewett, Laura M. 2008. *A Delicate Dance. Autoethnography, Curriculum, and the Semblance of Intimacy*. New York: Peter Lang.

Jupp, J.C. 2012, April. On the Internationalization of Curriculum: Toward Cosmopolitan Sensibilities. Paper presented at American Educational Research Association, Vancouver, British Columbia, Canada.

Kimmel, Michael S. 1996. *Manhood in America: A Cultural History*. New York: Free Press

Kliebard, Herbert M. 2000 a. [1970] Persistent Issues in Historical Perspective. In *Curriculum Theorizing: The Reconceptualization*, edited by William F. Pinar (pp. 39–50). Troy, New York: Educator's International Press. First printed in *Educational Comment* (1970), 31–41.

Kliebard, Herbert M. 2000 b. [1970]Reappraisal: The Tyler Rationale. In *Curriculum Theorizing: The Reconceptualization*, edited by William F. Pinar (pp. 70–83). Troy, New York: Educator's International Press. First printed in *School Review* (1970), 259–272.

Kuhn, Thomas. 1962. *The Structure of Scientific Revolutions*. Chicago: University of Chicago Press.

LaCapra, Dominick. 2004. *History in Transit: Experience, Identity, Critical Theory*. Ithaca, New York: Cornell University Press.

La Corte, Rachel. 2011, December 14. Gregoire Urges Reforms for Education. Plan Would Change Way Teachers and Principals Are Evaluated. *The Bellingham Herald*, A9.

Ladd, Helen F. and Fiske, Edward B. 2011, December 12. Class Matters. Why Won't We Admit It? *The New York Times* Vol. CLXI (55, 617), A21.

DOI: 10.1057/9781137303424

Ladson-Billings, Gloria and Tate IV, William F. 1995. Toward a Critical Race Theory of Education. *Teachers College Record* 97 (1), 47–68.

Lather, Patti. 2007. *Getting Lost: Feminist Efforts toward a Double(d) Science.* Albany: State University of New York Press.

Lather, Patti. 2010. Response to Jennifer Gilbert: The Doubt Trouble of Passing on Curriculum Studies. In *Curriculum Studies Handbook: The Next Moment*, edited by Erik Malewski (73–100). New York: Routledge.

Latta, Margaret Macintyre. (in press). *Curricular Conversations. Play is the (Missing) Thing.* New York: Routledge.

Lau, Joyce. 2012, July 30. Thousands Protest in Hong Kong Against China's Move to Impose Curriculum. *The New York Times* CLXI (55, 848), A4.

Lenoir, Timothy. 1993. The Discipline of Nature and the Nature of Disciplines. In *Knowledges: Historical and Critical Studies in Disciplinarity* edited by Ellen Messer-Davidow, David R. Shumway, and David J. Sylvan (70–102). Charlottesville: University Press of Virginia.

Lewin, Tamar. 2012, March 29. Feedback From Students Becomes a Campus Staple, but Some Go Further. *The New York Times* Vol. CLXI (55,725), A18.

Lewin, Tamar. 2012, July 30. Senate Committee Report on For-Profit College Condemns Costs and Practices. *The New York Times* CLXI (55, 848), A12.

Li, Xin. 2010. Response to Hongyu Wang: Intersubjective Becoming and Curriculum Creativity as International Text: A Resonance. In *Curriculum Studies Handbook: The Next Moment*, edited by Erik Malewski (387–392). New York: Routledge.

Lowrey, Annie. 2011, January 6. A Study Links Good Teachers to Lasting Gain. *The New York Times* Vol. CLXI (55, 642), A1, A14.

Macdonald, James B. 1995. *Theory as a Prayerful Act: Collected Essays.* [Edited by Bradley Macdonald and introduced by William F. Pinar.] New York: Peter Lang.

Macedo, Elizabeth. 2011. Curriculum as Cultural Enunciation. In *Curriculum Studies in Brazil: Intellectual Histories, Present Circumstances*, edited by William F. Pinar (135–153). New York: Palgrave Macmillan.

Malewski, Erik (ed.). 2010. *Curriculum Studies Handbook: The Next Moment.* New York: Routledge.

Mayer, Susan Jean. 2012. *Classroom Discourse and Democracy. Making Meanings Together.* New York: Peter Lang.

DOI: 10.1057/9781137303424

Mercer, Kobena. 1994. *Welcome to the Jungle: New Positions in Black Cultural Studies*. New York: Routledge.

McKnight, Douglas. 2010. Critical Pedagogy and Despair: A Move toward Kierkegaard's Passionate Inwardness. In *Curriculum Studies Handbook: The Next Moment*, edited by Erik Malewski (500–516). New York: Routledge.

Miller, Janet L. 2005. *The Sound of Silence Breaking and Other Essays: Working the Tension in Curriculum Theory*. New York: Peter Lang.

Miller, Janet L. 2010. Response to Rubén A. Gaztambide-Fernández: Communities Without Consensus. In *Curriculum Studies Handbook: The Next Moment*, edited by Erik Malewski (95–100). New York: Routledge.

Moon, Seungho. 2011. Rethinking Culturally Responsive Teaching for New (Im)possibilities of Multicultural Curriculum Studies and Policy. *Multicultural Education Review*, 3 (2), 69–102.

Morris, Marla. 2001. *Holocaust and Curriculum*. Mahwah, New Jersey: Lawrence Erlbaum.

Morris, Marla. 2006. *Jewish Intellectuals and the University*. New York: Palgrave Macmillan.

Morris, Marla. 2008. *Teaching Through the Ill Body*. Rotterdam: Sense Publishers.

Morris, Marla. 2009. *On Not Being Able to Play*. Rotterdam: Sense Publishers.

Murray, Stuart J. 2010. Response to Stephanie Springgay and Debra Freedman: Making Sense of Touch: Phenomenology and the Place of Language in a Bodied Curriculum. In *Curriculum Studies Handbook: The Next Moment*, edited by Erik Malewski (240–243). New York: Routledge.

National Commission on Excellence in Education. 1983. *A Nation at Risk: The Imperative for Educational Reform*. Washington, DC: United States Department of Education.

Ng-A-Fook, Nicholas and Rottman, Jenn. (eds). 2012. *Rethinking Canadian Curriculum Studies*. New York: Palgrave Macmillan.

Paraskeva, João M. 2011. *Conflicts in Curriculum Theory: Challenging Hegemonic Epistemologies*. New York: Palgrave Macmillan.

Phillips, Anna M. 2012, April 16. Private Tutoring for Many Elementary School Pupils. *The New York Times* Vol. CLXI (55,743), A14, A15.

Pinar, William F. 1972. Working From Within. *Educational Leadership*, 29 (4), 329–331.

DOI: 10.1057/9781137303424

Pinar, William F. 2001. *The Gender of Racial Politics and Violence in American: Lynching, Prison Rape, and the Crisis of Masculinity.* New York: Peter Lang.

Pinar, William F. 2004. *What Is Curriculum Theory?* Mahwah, New Jersey: Lawrence Erlbaum.

Pinar, William F. 2006a. *The Synoptic Text Today and Other Essays: Curriculum Development after the Reconceptualization.* New York: Peter Lang.

Pinar, William F. 2006b. *Race, Religion and a Curriculum of Reparation.* New York: Palgrave Macmillan.

Pinar, William F. 2007. *Intellectual Advancement through Disciplinarity: Verticality and Horizontality in Curriculum Studies.* Rotterdam and Taipei: Sense Publishers.

Pinar, William F. 2008. Curriculum Theory Since 1950: Crisis, Reconceptualization, Internationalization. In *The Sage Handbook of Curriculum and Instruction,* edited by F. Michael Connelly, Ming Fang He, and JoAnn Phillion (491–513). Los Angeles: Sage.

Pinar, William F. (ed.). 2010. *Curriculum Studies in South Africa: Intellectual Histories, Present Circumstances.* New York: Palgrave Macmillan.

Pinar, William F. 2011a. *The Character of Curriculum Studies: Bildung, Currere, and the Recurring Question of the Subject.* New York: Palgrave Macmillan.

Pinar, William F. (ed.). 2011b. *Curriculum Studies in Brazil: Intellectual Histories, Present Circumstances.* New York: Palgrave Macmillan.

Pinar, William F. 2011c. Nationalism, Anti-Americanism, Canadian Identity. In *Curriculum in Today's World: Configuring Knowledge, Identities, Work and Politics,* edited by Lyn Yates and Madeleine Grumet (31–43). London: Routledge.

Pinar, William F. (ed.). 2011d. *Curriculum Studies in Mexico: Intellectual Histories, Present Circumstances.* New York: Palgrave Macmillan.

Pinar, William F. 2011e. Nationalism, Anti-Americanism, Canadian Identity. In *Curriculum in Today's World: Configuring Knowledge, Identities, Work and Politics,* edited by Lyn Yates and Madeleine Grumet (31–43). London: Routledge.

Pinar, William F. 2012. *What Is Curriculum Theory?* [Second edition.] New York: Routledge.

Pinar, William F. and Grumet, Madeleine R. 2006 (1976). *Toward a Poor Curriculum.* Troy, New York: Educator's International Press. [Originally published by Kendall/Hunt.]

DOI: 10.1057/9781137303424

Pinar, William F., Reynolds, William, Slattery, Patrick, and Taubman, Peter. 1995. *Understanding Curriculum*. New York: Peter Lang.

Posnock, Ross. 1998. *Color & Culture: Black writers and the Making of the Modern Intellectual*. Cambridge, Massachusetts: Harvard University Press.

Quinn, Molly. 2010. "No Room in the Inn"? The Question of Hospitality in the Post(Partum)-Labors of Curriculum Studies. In *Curriculum Studies Handbook: The Next Moment*, edited by Erik Malewski (101–117). New York: Routledge.

Roberts, David D. 1995. *Nothing but History: Reconstruction and Extremity after Metaphysics*. Berkeley and Los Angeles: University of California Press.

Radhakrishnan, R. 2008. *History, the Human, and the World Between*. Durham, North Carolina: Duke University Press.

Ravitch, Diane. 2000. *Left Back: A Century of Battles over School Reform*. New York: Simon and Schuster.

Ravitch, Diane. 2012, July 12. In Mitt Romney's Schoolroom. *The New York Review of Books*, Vol. LIX, No. 12, 38, 40.

Rich, Motoko. 2012, July 24. Enrollment Off in Big Districts, Forcing Layoffs. Steady 5-Year Decline. *The New York Times* CLXI (55, 842), A1, A3.

Rich, Motoko. 2012, July 27. States With Education Waivers Offer Varied Goals. *The New York Times* CLXI (55, 845), A14.

Richtel, Matt. 2011, November 5. Silicon Valley Wows Education, and Woos Them. *The New York Times* Vol. CLXI (55,580), A1, B7.

Richtel, Matt. 2012, January 4. Teachers Resist High-Tech Push in Idaho Schools. *The New York Times* Vol. CLXI (55, 640), A1, B4.

Riley-Taylor, Elaine. 2010. Reconceiving Ecology: Diversity, Language, and Horizons of the Possible. In *Curriculum Studies Handbook: The Next Moment*, edited by Erik Malewski (286–298). New York: Routledge.

Robinson, Marilynne. 2010. *Absence of Mind: The Dispelling of Inwardness from the Modern Myth of the Self*. New Haven, Connecticut: Yale University Press.

Rodriguez, Alberto J. and Kitchen, Richard S. (eds). 2004. *Preparing Mathematics and Science Teachers for Diverse Classrooms*. Mahwah, New Jersey: Lawrence Erlbaum.

Salvio, Paula. 1998. On Using the Literacy Portfolio to Prepare Teachers for "Willful World Traveling." In *Curriculum: Toward New Identities*, edited by William F. Pinar (41–74). New York: Garland.

DOI: 10.1057/9781137303424

Salvio, Paula M. 2007. *Anne Sexton: Teacher of Weird Abundance*. Albany: State University of New York Press.

Sandlin, Jennifer A., Schultz, Brian D., and Burdick, Jake. (eds). 2010. *Handbook of Public Pedagogy: Education and Learning beyond Schooling*. New York: Routledge.

Santos, Fernanda. 2012, March 8. Depth of Teacher Morale Is Shown in New Survey. *The New York Times* Vol. CLXI (55,704), A15.

Santos, Fernanda and Gebeloff, Robert. 2012, February 25. City Releases Ratings of 18,000 Teachers; Acknowledges Limitations of Data. *The New York Times* Vol. CLXI (55,692), A15.

Santos, Fernanda and Phillips, Anna M. 2012, February 27. After Release of Teacher Ratings, a Rallying Cry Emerges for the Union. *The New York Times* Vol. CLXI (55,694), A13, A15.

Saul, John Ralston. 2008. *A Fair Country: Telling Truths about Canada*. Toronto: Viking Canada.

Saul, Stephanie. 2011, December 13. Profits and Questions at Online Charter Schools. Parents Get to Choose, but Standards Slip and Scores Suffer. *The New York Times* Vol. CLXI (55, 618), A1, A18-A19.

Schwab, Joseph J. 1970. *The Practical: A Language for Curriculum*. Washington, DC: National Education Association.

Schwarz, Alan. 2011, August 8. Atlanta School Year Begins Amid a Testing Scandal. *The New York Times* CLX (55,491), A10.

Schwarz, Alan. 2012, February 13. Mooresville's Shining Example (It's Not Just About the Laptops): With Computers, Tapping Into Emotions for Success. *The New York Times* Vol. CLXI (55,680), A10, A12.

Silverman, Rachel Emma. 2012, January 31. Study: Face Time Benefits Preteens. *The Wall Street Journal*, Vol. CCLIX (No. 24), D2.

Slattery, Patrick. 2010. Response to Ugena Whitlock: Curriculum as a Queer Southern Place: Reflections on Ugena Whitlock's "Jesus Died for NASCAR Fans." In *Curriculum Studies Handbook: The Next Moment*, edited by Erik Malewski (281–285). New York: Routledge.

Snaza, Nathan. 2010. Thirteen Theses on the Question of State in Curriculum Studies. In *Curriculum Studies Handbook: The Next Moment*, edited by Erik Malewski (43–56). New York: Routledge.

Spector, Hannah. 2011. [Invited essay review] The Question of Cosmopolitanism: An Essay Review. *Education Review*. 14 (2), 1–14. url: http://www.edrev.info/essays/v14n2.pdf

Spring, Joel. 2012. *Education Networks: Power, Wealth, Cyberspace, and the Digital Mind*. New York: Routledge.

DOI: 10.1057/9781137303424

Springgay, Stephanie and Freeman, Debra. 2010. Sleeping with Cake and Other Touchable Encounters: Performing a Bodies Curriculum. In *Curriculum Studies Handbook: The Next Moment*, edited by Erik Malewski (228–239). New York: Routledge.

Springgay, Stephanie, Irwin, Rita L., Leggo, Carl, and Gouzouasis, Peter. (eds). 2008. *Being with A/r/tography*. Rotterdam and Tapei: Sense Publishers.

Stanley, Darren and Kelly Young. (eds). 2011. *Contemporary Studies in Canadian Curriculum: Principles, Portraits and Practices*. Calgary, Alberta, Canada: Detselig.

Taliaferro-Baszile, Denise. 2010. In Ellisonian Eyes, What Is Curriculum Theory? In *Curriculum Studies Handbook: The Next Moment*, edited by Erik Malewski (483–495). New York: Routledge.

Taubman, Peter M. 1982. Gender and Curriculum: Discourse and the Politics of Sexuality. *Journal of Curriculum Theorizing*, 4 (1), 12–87.

Taubman, Peter M. 2009. *Teaching by Numbers: Deconstructing the Discourse of Standards and Accountability in Education*. New York: Routledge.

Taubman, Peter M. 2011. *Disavowed Knowledge*. New York: Routledge.

Tavernise, Sabrina. 2012, February 10. Rich and Poor Further Apart in Education. *The New York Times* Vol. CLXI (55,677), A1, A3.

Tom, Alan. 1984. *Teaching as a Moral Craft*. New York: Longman.

Tröhler, Daniel. 2006. The "Kingdom of God on Earth" and Early Chicago Pragmatism. *Educational Theory* 56 (1), 89–105.

Tröhler, Daniel. 2011. *Languages of Education. Protestant Legacies, National Identities, and Global Aspirations*. New York: Routledge.

Trueit, Donna. (ed.). 2012. *Pragmatism, Postmodernism, Complexity Theory: The Fascinating Imaginative Realm of William E. Doll, Jr*. New York: Routledge.

Turner, Dorie. 2011, January 3. 2011 School Year Marred By Test Cheating Scandals Across U.S. *The Bellingham Herald*, B5.

Tyler, Ralph W. 1949. *Basic Principles of Curriculum and Instruction*. Chicago: University of Chicago Press.

Van Deburg, William L. 1997. *Black Camelot: African-American Culture Heroes in Their Times, 1960–1980*. Chicago: University of Chicago Press.

Wang, Hongyu. 2004. *The Call from the Stranger on a Journey Home: Curriculum in a Third Space*. New York: Peter Lang.

Wang, Hongyu. 2010. Intimate Revolt and Third Possibilities: Cocreating a Creative Curriculum. In *Curriculum Studies Handbook: The Next Moment*, edited by Erik Malewski (374–386). New York: Routledge.

DOI: 10.1057/9781137303424

Watson, Alexander John. 2007. *Marginal Man: The Dark Vision of Harold Innis.* Toronto: University of Toronto Press.

Weaver, John A. 2010. The Posthuman Condition: A Complicated Conversation. In *Curriculum Studies Handbook: The Next Moment,* edited by Erik Malewski (190–200). New York: Routledge.

Whitlock, Ugena. 2007. *This Corner of Canaan. Curriculum Studies of Place and the Reconstruction of the South.* New York: Peter Lang.

Whitlock, Ugena. 2010. Jesus Died for NASCAR Fans: The Significance of Rural Formations of Queerness to Curriculum Studies. In *Curriculum Studies Handbook: The Next Moment,* edited by Erik Malewski (265–280). New York: Routledge.

Willinsky, John. 2006. *The Access Principle: The Case for Open Access to Research and Scholarship.* Cambridge, Massachusetts: MIT Press.

Winerip, Michael. 2012, February 27. An Unsettling Sight Amid a Federal Inquiry. *The New York Times* Vol. CLXI (55,694), A10.

Winerip, Michael. 2012, March 19. Racial Lens Used to Cull Curriculum in Arizona. *The New York Times* Vol. CLXI (55,715), A8, A12.

Winfield, Annie. 2010. Eugenic Ideology and Historical Osmosis. In *Curriculum Studies Handbook: The Next Moment,* edited by Erik Malewski (142–157). New York: Routledge.

Wooten, Sara Carrigan. 2011. Whispers in the Halls. *Journal of Curriculum Theorizing* 27 (3), 317–324.

Yates, Lyn and Grumet, Madeleine. (eds). 2011. *Curriculum in Today's World: Configuring Knowledge, Identities, Work and Politics.* London: Routledge.

DOI: 10.1057/9781137303424

Index

DOI: 10.1057/9781137303424

DOI: 10.1057/9781137303424

DOI: 10.1057/9781137303424

DOI: 10.1057/9781137303424

DOI: 10.1057/9781137303424

DOI: 10.1057/9781137303424

DOI: 10.1057/9781137303424

DOI: 10.1057/9781137303424

DOI: 10.1057/9781137303424

DOI: 10.1057/9781137303424

DOI: 10.1057/9781137303424

DOI: 10.1057/9781137303424

DOI: 10.1057/9781137303424

DOI: 10.1057/9781137303424

CPSIA information can be obtained at www.ICGtesting.com
Printed in the USA
LVOW120909150413

329114LV00002B/25/P

9 781137 303417